Welcome!

from our fierce founder

Welcome to issue 31 of *Fierce Truths Magazine*! It's our 3rd birthday, and in this issue, we get to celebrate and reflect on the incredible journey we have taken over the last three years. What started as a singular vision has blossomed into so much more! I am grateful to every reader and collaborator who has been a part of this transformative ride.

In this very special issue, we have chosen to explore our magazine's roots by spotlighting its birth and creation. So - I sat down for my very own interview to discuss the story behind *Fierce Truths Magazine*. It is an intimate peek into our humble beginnings, the hurdles we overcame, and the passion that fueled our growth.

Additionally, we had the immense privilege of interviewing the remarkable Karen Ridder. Her mission to create peace and healing in a chaotic and fragmented world is heartwarming and inspirational. Her story will touch your soul and remind you of the power of purpose and following your truth.

We are also thrilled to hear some personal stories from leading experts in the fields of spirituality, wellness, and personal growth. Their wisdom and knowledge will undoubtedly enrich your journey of self-discovery.

Our intent with every issue of *Fierce Truths Magazine* is to inspire, transform and spiritually educate you. Giving you the tools you need to activate that best version of yourself. So, I **Hope that one of our articles will remind you of how extraordinary you are, and how incredible your life can be.**

With fierce love,

KIM BLEEZE
Founder & Vision Holder
FIERCE TRUTHS MAGAZINE

Follow us on social media
@fiercetruthsmagazine

CONTENTS

Monthly Musing 98

Monthly advice with our fierce team of experts!

OUR TEAM

Editorial

Kim Bleeze
Editor-in-chief | Creative Director | Lay-out Design

Analee Davie
Proof-reader

Andrew Karabatos
Layout Consultant

Our Fierce Experts

Karina Barca
Empowered Healing

Tui Te Kiri
Spirit & Soul

Leila Verban
Movement Matters

Paul Quinton
Channeling a New Earth

Jasmine Gatt
Self-Love and WOO

Narelle Clyde
Sacred Self Expressioon

Melanie Oborne
The Science in Spirituality

Guest Contributors

Jess Moss
Creating Healing Environments

Karen Ridder
Interview: Divine Mission of Peace and Healing

Kylie Attwell
From Anxiety and Depression to Living with Purpose

Jackie Norman
The Most Important Journey of All

Farita Khambatta
Spirituality, Healing and Hope

Kim Bleeze
Feature Interview: Behind the Pages

Staff

Jasmine Robante
Outreach Manager
Social Media Engagement

Contact

Management & Advertising
fierce@fiercetruthsmagazine.com

Support & Inquiries
ask@fiercetruthsmagazine.com

Find yourself...
by getting lost

© Fierce Truths Magazine
IMAGE CREDIT @RADARAN.X.ADOBE.COM

We love
Sharing the **LOVE**

Conscious
RELATIONSHIPS

Nurturing Connections Through **Mindful Communication**

Maintaining meaningful relationships can sometimes feel like a challenge in today's fast-paced world, where technology has become integral to our lives. We find ourselves constantly distracted by screens, bombarded with information, and struggling to find genuine connections with those around us.

However, by embracing the principles of conscious relationships and practising mindful communication, we can create deeper and more fulfilling connections with our loved ones.

What are Conscious Relationships

They are relationships in which both partners actively engage in personal growth and self-awareness while fostering a deep connection with each other. These relationships are built on a foundation of mutual respect, trust, and understanding. Mindful communication plays a vital role in nurturing these connections, allowing individuals to express themselves authentically and empathetically.

Mindful communication involves being fully present and attentive during conversations, listening with an open heart and without judgment. It requires us to let go of distractions and truly engage with our partners. By actively listening, we validate their emotions and experiences, fostering an environment of trust and empathy. Mindful communication is a two-way street; it requires both partners to be fully engaged in the process. Conflicts are resolved more effectively when both individuals practice mindful communication and allow relationships to flourish healthily.

One key aspect of mindful communication is self-awareness. Understanding our own emotions, triggers, and communication patterns is crucial for effective and authentic expression. By recognising our own feelings and needs, we can communicate them clearly and honestly to our partners. This self-awareness allows us to avoid projecting our insecurities or frustrations onto our loved ones, leading to more open and constructive conversations.

Another vital component of mindful communication is empathy. Empathy involves putting ourselves in our partner's shoes and striving to understand their perspective and emotions. It requires us to suspend judgment and truly listen to their experiences. When we empathise with our partners, we create an environment encouraging vulnerability and fostering deeper emotional connections.

Practising mindfulness outside of direct communication is also essential for nurturing conscious relationships. Mindfulness involves being fully present in the moment and observing our thoughts and emotions without judgment. By cultivating mindfulness individually, we enhance our ability to show up fully for ourselves and in our relationships. Mindfulness helps us recognise our reactions and triggers, allowing us to respond consciously rather than reactively. It also enables us to recognise when we need to take a step back and take care of ourselves, ensuring that we approach our relationships from a place of emotional stability and well-being.

In addition to mindfulness, setting clear boundaries is crucial for maintaining healthy and conscious relationships. Boundaries allow individuals to express their needs and limits, creating a safe space for both partners to thrive. By clearly communicating and respecting each other's boundaries, couples foster a sense of security and mutual understanding. Practising gratitude and appreciation is another powerful tool for nurturing conscious relationships. Expressing gratitude for our partners and the positive aspects of our relationship fosters a sense of connection and appreciation. Taking the time to acknowledge and celebrate each other's strengths and efforts strengthens the bond between partners, creating a nurturing and loving environment.

Finally, conflict resolution is an integral part of any relationship. In conscious relationships, conflicts are seen as opportunities for growth and understanding. Instead of avoiding or suppressing disagreements, couples approach conflicts with curiosity and a willingness to learn. Conflicts can be transformed into opportunities for deeper connection and mutual growth by actively listening, empathising, and finding common ground.

Conscious relationships require ongoing effort and commitment. They demand that we remain mindful, communicative, and open-hearted. However, the rewards are immense. By nurturing connections through mindful and conscious communication, we create relationships that are built on a foundation of trust, authenticity, and deep emotional bonds. These relationships provide a haven in a fast-paced world, allowing us to grow individually and together and navigate life's challenges with a sense of security and support.

In conscious relationships, partners understand that growth and personal development are ongoing journeys. They encourage each other to pursue individual passions, dreams, and goals while nurturing shared dreams and aspirations. By supporting each other's personal growth, couples in conscious relationships create an environment that fosters personal fulfilment and allows each partner to thrive.

Furthermore, conscious relationships emphasise the importance of shared values and shared experiences. Couples engage in activities and rituals that deepen their connection and create lasting memories. Whether travelling together, engaging in shared hobbies, or simply spending quality time, these shared experiences strengthen the bond between partners and create a sense of unity.

While often blamed for creating distance in relationships, technology can also be utilised mindfully to enhance communication and connection. Couples in conscious relationships establish healthy boundaries around technology use and consciously prioritise face-to-face interactions. They understand the value of being fully present with each other and utilising technology to stay connected rather than allowing it to become a barrier.

It is important to note that conscious relationships are not immune to challenges. Like any relationship, they require effort, patience, and understanding. However, the

foundation of open communication and mindfulness built within conscious relationships provides a solid framework for navigating difficulties.

Partners in conscious relationships approach challenges as opportunities to learn and grow together rather than allowing them to create distance or resentment.

In a world that often promotes superficial connections and instant gratification, conscious relationships offer an alternative path to lasting fulfilment and love. They require us to slow down, listen deeply, and be present with ourselves and our partners. Through mindful communication, empathy, self-awareness, and the cultivation of shared values, conscious relationships create a space where individuals can truly be seen, heard, and understood.

As we continue to navigate the complexities of modern life, investing in our relationships consciously becomes increasingly essential. By prioritising mindful communication, we can break free from the distractions surrounding us and cultivate genuine connections with our loved ones. So, let us embrace the principles of conscious relationships and nurture our connections through mindful communication, creating relationships that enrich our lives and contribute to our overall well-being.

Practice Active Listening

01 Make a conscious effort to be fully present during conversations. Avoid distractions like phones or laptops, maintain eye contact, and truly listen to your partner's words. Avoid interrupting or formulating responses in your mind before they have finished speaking.

Cultivate Self-Awareness

02 Take the time to reflect on your own emotions, triggers, and communication patterns. Understand how your thoughts and emotions influence your interactions with your partner. This self-awareness allows you to communicate more authentically and take responsibility for your reactions.

Foster Empathy

03 Put yourself in your partner's shoes and strive to understand their perspective. Practice active empathy by listening attentively, validating their emotions, and expressing understanding. Empathy helps create a safe space for vulnerability and deepens emotional connections.

Practice Mindfulness

04 Cultivate mindfulness in your daily life by engaging in activities that promote present-moment awareness, such as meditation, deep breathing exercises, or mindful walks. This practice allows you to respond consciously rather than reactively in your interactions with your partner.

Set Clear Boundaries

05 Establish open and honest communication about your personal boundaries and encourage your partner to do the same. Respect each other's limits and needs, creating a safe space where both partners feel heard and understood.

Express Gratitude and Appreciation

06

Regularly express gratitude for your partner and the positive aspects of your relationship. Acknowledge and celebrate each other's strengths and efforts. Cultivating an attitude of gratitude fosters a sense of connection and appreciation.

Transform Conflicts into Opportunities for Growth

07

Approach conflicts with curiosity and a willingness to understand your partner's perspective. Engage in open, honest dialogue, actively listen, and seek common ground—view conflicts as opportunities for deeper understanding and mutual growth.

Prioritise Quality Time

08

Make a conscious effort to spend quality time together without distractions. Plan activities or rituals that foster connection and create lasting memories. Prioritising uninterrupted face-to-face interactions strengthens the bond between partners.

Communicate Your Needs and Desires

09

Be open and honest about your needs, desires, and concerns. Clearly communicate what you require from the relationship and encourage your partner to do the same. This promotes understanding and allows for the fulfilment of each other's needs.

Practice Forgiveness and Compassion

10

Understand that you and your partner are imperfect and may make mistakes. Cultivate a mindset of forgiveness and compassion, allowing space for growth and healing. Let go of past resentments and approach conflicts with a willingness to find a resolution.

Always remember...
Cultivating conscious relationships through mindful communication and nurturing connections can create relationships that bring joy, fulfilment, and growth to our lives.

Fill your body

With love

Creating
HEALING ENVIRONMENTS

LIFE AFTER DOMESTIC VIOLENCE

A PERSONAL STORY

By Jessie Moss

I was addicted to the loop of instability. I unconsciously chased unsafe situations. Even as I became more aware, the poor me attitude quickly brought me to the same situations time and time again, just showing up in so many different types of people, different ways on different days. It was getting old.

Eventually, I was so puzzled by the heartache I endured that I wanted to address the pattern. I realised what triggered me were the things that were keeping me in the loop of victimhood and fear-based choices that only amplified my situation well after getting out of an abusive marriage. I chose it without knowing just because it was so familiar.

I found the dysfunction I was running from and how I would declare never accepting certain treatment for myself ever again was, in fact, the sneaky thing I had to watch for because I was so used to operating in the world in a state of survival. Looking back now, I found I was constantly seeking comfort from the ones who hurt me most, which was a learnt behaviour.

My chaotic state of living in struggle meant I would numb myself with alcohol and avoid the deeper issues that were too painful to see by keeping myself busy. I never rested because it was uncomfortable to be still. I blamed myself, which kept me stuck for many years after getting out of my tangle with domestic violence. I felt I was not fully free, but somehow I also felt that's what I wanted so badly.

I understood so much with my mind, but my body wasn't speaking the same language. Turns out, when I spoke to my body during experiencing anxiety and told it with words, "Just calm down, stop being silly", it actually made the anxiety so much worse because I was pushing this part of myself away, shaming it and telling it that it isn't valid to respond like that.

> ## I had to get to know myself, learn why my stories were keeping me stuck, and how they shaped me.

Unworthiness would wake with me every morning; I'd pick her up and piggyback her around everywhere, listening to the things she would whisper to me like "You can't do that" or "You aren't good enough, so don't even try". This part of myself was heavy with responsibility. Naturally, I was unaware I had a part so unloved, unwanted, and who felt she didn't belong in the world, but I carried her around like the weight of the world on my shoulders.

I noticed this part of myself through EMDR therapy, where I addressed the burden she was carrying. I noticed it wasn't my fault, and the things that were happening to me were because I still believed what I absorbed from childhood. All the times I was never chosen or excluded for being different brought a people-pleasing quality to the cycle I was in, and I had been moulded into believing if I did things at the cost of myself, then people would want me around, and they would choose me.

All the things that led to having complex trauma became really apparent to me when I was 29 years old, in the midst of a divorce and a time I had to fight for my life. It wasn't until I hit rock bottom that I realised trauma was steering my life with a CPTSD diagnosis at age 30. After this time of realisation, I learned about the brain and cultivated acceptance around my beliefs as I

changed them. It was a long journey back to health through small choices.

It is still a lot of work even today. I am now 37. The biggest struggles I find now are in relationships, sometimes finding myself wondering if I am safe, having trouble sometimes staying open, and catching myself when responses arise. I can sometimes feel there is so much work always being done like it will never end, and the biggest thing I forget to do is to play, rest and experience joy.

One of the biggest learnings for me was accepting I had CPTSD. I could no longer ignore it or just continue controlling my life around survival mode and only opening to where I was comfortable. I was missing out. I wanted more for myself.

I learnt what my triggers were, which include not feeling wanted, people not following through with what they say, staying in any situation where I am uncomfortable and unable to speak up, and any type of gaslighting or sense of manipulation sets me off to the point I can have a response. It has shifted from the age of 29, where I was being stalked, harassed and threatened - it's less physical safety now, and I find it to be more emotional work and nervous system regulation when I am uncomfortable, which I need to do now.

It is helpful for me to recognise my past abuse and remind myself I am not there. I now have created a support network with people that understand me, which is one of the most soothing and helpful things to feel.

It is important that I hold myself accountable to not project my past into the moments I am experiencing new situations, and I do this by asking myself, "Is this true"? This helps me to zoom out and see if I've become blended with fear, anxiety, doubt or any kind of protective coping mechanisms.

I take full responsibility for nourishing my body so I can do this work. I have devoted myself to the practice of yoga, meditating, receiving frequent bodywork, quitting alcohol and eating healthy. By knowing the things that trigger me, I can choose better for myself and work within my capacity as I heal.

Learning to speak about what my needs are have also been a huge help, but first, I needed a safe space to do that in.

I have found that I cannot heal anything or stay on a path of awareness when I am not in a supportive environment. I also acknowledge that I am working my way towards a secure attachment style where I believe when someone doesn't know how to support or validate the responses or emotions I am having, it doesn't mean I am too much or that I have to heal it alone. I still know I can be triggered, and I know my limits while I work on creating stability within myself.

When I choose situations or life happens, and I am thrown something I wasn't expecting, I try not to be too hard on myself as I recover. There is no time limit on recovery. I take a pause. I do things that help me feel calm, I go to therapy, I let my emotions out, I journal, when I feel ready, I lean into support and all the things that help orient me back to my life right now.

It is so easy to go back; the victim is so familiar, and sometimes, when things are good, it calls me so loudly that I cannot hear anything else. To know my survival tendencies and then, when calm and present, telling people close to me about them so they can help me catch them helps me to create an environment for myself where I can live more peacefully.

I still have responses to new stimulus, and new challenges that come through other people's lack of boundaries. Anytime I may not feel understood or safe —- no matter what it is or how big or small it is —- it is always an opportunity for me to understand myself a little deeper, and to choose healing.

I see my past as this constant reminder to choose.

Choosing places me in the driver's seat where I can thrive despite anything that happens, that things can still happen, and I can say no, choose peace, remove myself and come back to regulation by practising the tools I now have.

It's important to me I walk my path with enough courage to choose peace and not go into self-sabotaging, addictions or the cut-and-run attitude. I know none of it serves me, and the more I flex the trust muscle to the life of ease I have acquired, I remind myself, "This is my new normal".

**I am here.
I am no longer there.
I might go back, but I let it be brief.
I choose again.**

Jessie Moss is an intuitive awakening facilitator and Author of the book *Open*. Jessie teaches you to transform through the higher frequency of your heart, align all areas of your life from within, and be open to the highest possibilities of love and liberation. Based in Noosa, holding retreats, online courses and events that heal the mind, body and soul. Meeting people in the space of transition and change.

Learn more about Jessie: www.jessiemoss.com

you
a
ena

e
ugh

EARTH CHAKRAS

AND CONNECTING TO THE ENERGY GRID

Our world is a tapestry of interconnected energies flowing through every living being and object. Just as we humans have chakras that serve as energy centres within our bodies, the Earth itself has its own energy centres known as Earth Chakras, which are found in various locations worldwide. These powerful focal points of energy influence the planet's well-being and profoundly impact our lives; we just don't know it.

WHAT ARE EARTH CHAKRAS?

Earth Chakras, also known as Gaia Chakras, are considered energetic vortices that serve as centres of power, similar to the human chakra system. These chakras are said to channel and distribute vital life force energy throughout the planet, forming an intricate grid that connects all living beings and natural elements. It is believed that these Earth Chakras play a vital role in maintaining the balance and harmony of the Earth.

WHERE ARE THE EARTH CHAKRAS LOCATED?

The locations of the Earth Chakras have been a subject of exploration and debate among spiritual practitioners and scholars for many years. There are various theories and interpretations regarding the exact placement of these chakras, but a commonly accepted framework identifies seven primary Earth Chakras. These are typically associated with significant geographical sites and landmarks with immense spiritual, historical, or cultural significance.

Mount Shasta
ROOT CHAKRA

1 Mount Shasta, California, USA: Known as the Root Chakra of the Earth, Mount Shasta is associated with grounding and stability.

2 Lake Titicaca, Peru/Bolivia: Considered the Sacral Chakra, this sacred lake represents the seat of creation and fertility.

3 Uluru-Kata Tjuta, Australia: Often called the Solar Plexus Chakra (Australia's heart chakra), this iconic sandstone formation symbolizes personal power and transformation.

Lake Titicaca
SACRAL CHAKRA

Uluru-Kata Tjuta
SOLAR PLEXUS (Australia-Heart Chakra)

Glastonbury
HEART CHAKRA

Pyramid of Giza
THROAT CHAKRA

4 Glastonbury, England: Thought to be the Earth's Heart Chakra, Glastonbury holds a deep spiritual resonance and is associated with love and healing.

5 Great Pyramid of Giza, Egypt: Representing the Throat Chakra, this ancient wonder embodies communication, wisdom, and self-expression.

6 Kuh-e Malek Siah, Iran: Known as the Third Eye Chakra, this mountain is believed to enhance intuition and spiritual insight. (Not pictured)

7 Mount Kailash, Tibet: Considered the Crown Chakra, this revered peak is associated with enlightenment, divine connection, and spiritual awakening.

Mount Kailash
CROWN CHAKRA

WHAT DO THE DIFFERENT EARTH CHAKRAS REPRESENT?

Each Earth Chakra holds unique qualities and symbolism, corresponding to the seven main chakras in the human body. By understanding the representations of these Earth Chakras, we can deepen our connection with the Earth and align our energies with their specific attributes.

For example, the Root Chakra represents stability, grounding, and physical well-being. At the same time, the Sacral Chakra embodies creativity, passion, and emotional balance. Moving up, the Solar Plexus Chakra represents personal power and confidence, and the Heart Chakra signifies love, compassion, and unity. The Throat Chakra embodies clear communication and authentic expression, while the Third Eye Chakra relates to intuition, inner vision, and spiritual awareness. Finally, the Crown Chakra represents higher consciousness, enlightenment, and divine connection.

WHAT CAN KNOWING ABOUT THE EARTH CHAKRAS ADD TO YOUR LIFE?

Deepening our understanding of the Earth's Chakras can bring profound benefits to our lives. By recognizing the interconnectedness of all living beings and the planet, we can develop a more profound sense of belonging and purpose. Knowing about the Earth Chakras invites us to become more mindful of the energy that flows within and around us. This awareness allows us to harmonize our own chakras with the corresponding Earth Chakras, creating a powerful synergy that promotes balance, healing, and spiritual growth.

Moreover, understanding the Earth Chakras can foster a profound reverence and respect for the planet. We begin to recognize that our actions and choices directly impact the Earth's energetic well-being. By aligning ourselves with the Earth Chakras, we can consciously contribute to restoring and preserving the planet's energetic equilibrium.

How Can We Work With the Earth Chakras Remotely?

While physically visiting the Earth Chakras may not be feasible for everyone, working with these energy centres remotely is possible. Distance is not a barrier when it comes to energy work and spiritual connection. Here are a few practices you can explore to engage with the Earth Chakras from wherever you are:

Crystal Healing:

Crystals are powerful energy conduits and can aid in working with Earth Chakras remotely. Choose crystals that resonate with the specific chakra you are connecting with. Place them on your body or in your surroundings during meditation or energy healing practices.

Sending Healing Energy:

Use the power of your intention and visualization to send healing energy to the Earth Chakra. Envision vibrant, pure energy flowing into the chakra, revitalizing and harmonizing its energetic flow.

Meditation and Visualization:

Set aside quiet time to meditate and visualize the Earth Chakra you wish to connect with. Envision yourself immersed in its energy, absorbing its qualities and allowing it to cleanse, heal, and empower you.

Earth Connection Rituals:

Engage in rituals that deeply connect nature and the Earth. This could include activities such as walking barefoot on the Earth, gardening, or spending time in natural environments.

Intentions and Affirmations:

Formulate positive intentions and affirmations that align with the specific attributes of the Earth Chakra you are focusing on. Repeat these affirmations regularly, sending your intentions out into the energetic grid of the Earth.

Earth Chakras offer a profound opportunity to deepen our connection with the planet and tap into the vast energy reservoirs surrounding us. Understanding their locations, symbolism, and attributes allows us to align ourselves with these powerful energy centres and transform our lives. Whether through physical visits or remote practices, engaging with the Earth Chakras allows us to become co-creators of a more harmonious and balanced world. **It invites us to deepen our energetic exploration and healing for ourselves and the planet we call home.**

Live

ON YOUR OWN
TIME

• BE YOUR O

beau

WN KIND OF•

tiful

A DIVINE MISSION OF Peace AND HEALING

Karen Ridder's Journey to Harmonize Lives with the Ancient Art of Jin Shin Jyutsu

AN INTERVIEW

Karen Ridder, a devoted mother, and passionate practitioner of Jin Shin Jyutsu, has dedicated her life to spreading the transformative power of this ancient healing art. With a deep belief in its ability to bring harmony and well-being to individuals, Karen's mission is to make Jin Shin Jyutsu a household name, empowering people to take control of their health and lead more fulfilled lives.

Like many whose path is to create a ripple of impact in the world, Karen's journey began with a personal crisis that turned her life upside down. Her son's diagnosis of Hypogammaglobulinemia, an immune disorder that threatened his well-being. Overwhelmed with fear and anxiety, Karen embarked on a path that led her to Jin Shin Jyutsu. She found solace and a deep sense of hope through this divine encounter.

Describing her journey, Karen explains, *"With Jin Shin Jyutsu, I had this belief and feeling deep down that we were always going to be okay. It was a divine, guided happenstance that I was introduced to this beautiful philosophy. I truly believe it's my divine mission to make Jin Shin Jyutsu a household name."*

Jin Shin Jyutsu is often likened to acupuncture but without the use of needles. It involves using the hands to apply gentle pressure on specific points, known as "safety energy locks," to release blocked energy and restore balance. By reconnecting individuals to their perfect life source, this ancient practice can potentially harmonize physical, mental, emotional, and spiritual aspects of one's being.

Karen emphasizes the simplicity and effectiveness of Jin Shin Jyutsu, stating, *"It's so easy and gentle, yet amazingly effective and transformative. If individuals devoted just a few minutes each day to self-help practices, the quality of their lives and the world would improve significantly."*

One of the remarkable aspects of Jin Shin Jyutsu is its accessibility. While seeking professional sessions with practitioners can be beneficial, the art also encourages self-help practices. Karen highlights the abundance of online resources, including guided meditations and self-help videos on platforms like YouTube. These resources allow individuals to experience the healing benefits of Jin Shin Jyutsu at their own convenience, fostering a sense of empowerment and well-being.

From a physical standpoint, Jin Shin Jyutsu has the potential to enhance the body's immune system, supporting overall health. Karen affirms, *"While Jin Shin Jyutsu is not a substitute for medical care, regular self-help practices can reduce the need for frequent doctor visits and medication intake. It promotes better health outcomes and helps individuals make choices aligned with their highest well-being."*

Beyond physical well-being, Jin Shin Jyutsu addresses mental, emotional, and spiritual aspects of one's being. In today's tumultuous world, where anxiety and stress are prevalent, Jin Shin Jyutsu offers a path to tranquillity and peace. Karen's personal experiences and those of her clients bear witness to the art's ability to alleviate anxiety, depression, and anger. By harmonizing emotions and restoring balance, individuals can make empowered decisions based on love and compassion rather than trauma or reactive patterns, thus helping individuals overcome anxiety and temper issues to relieve symptoms of chronic conditions. The art's potential for positive change is remarkable.

With her unwavering commitment to her mission, Karen understands the importance of sharing Jin Shin Jyutsu with a broader audience. Recognizing the need for greater awareness and accessibility, she has enlisted a PR person's help to promote her work and spread the message of Jin Shin Jyutsu. Through interviews, articles, and various platforms, Karen aims to reach those who may benefit from this transformative practice.

Karen's purpose is to become a change-maker and leader in the field of holistic healing, and has not without its challenges.

As a devoted mother and caregiver for many years, she put her children's needs before her own. However, as her children grew older and more independent, she realized it was now her time to give back to the world and fulfil her divine mission.

Opening a professional practice and continuously deepening her knowledge and skills in Jin Shin Jyutsu, Karen has honed her ability to bring healing and transformation to those who seek her help. Through sessions with clients, she witnesses firsthand the profound shifts and improvements in their lives as they find balance, peace, and well-being.

Karen Ridder is a beacon of light, and in a time marked by global challenges and increasing anxiety and stress levels, she believes that the world needs Jin Shin Jyutsu now more than ever. Her vision for the future is one where people take control of their health, find inner harmony, and make choices aligned with their highest well-being. By incorporating Jin Shin Jyutsu into their lives, individuals can experience physical healing and a sense of empowerment, self-care, and compassion.

By sharing her divine mission with the world, Karen's compassionate heart and unwavering commitment empowers individuals and fosters a harmonious and loving existence for all willing to learn about Jin Shin Jyutsu. She reminds us that healing begins within, and by embracing this ancient art, we can create a ripple effect of peace, love, and well-being that reverberates throughout the world.

Karen's journey from devoted mother to change-maker serves as an inspiring reminder that we all have the power to transform our lives and the lives of others. Her story serves as a testament to the power of embracing one's divine mission and following the heart's calling, ultimately leading to a life of purpose, fulfilment, and the ability to create positive change in the world because we all have the ability to shape a more harmonious and peaceful world for all.

Karen, what's your fierce truth?

"I am all peace and love, but I find that throughout my life,
I've let people treat me in ways that weren't very kind.

I'm 55 now, and part of my journey is standing up for myself
more and only allowing people in my life that make me feel
loved and valued."

Yourself

There seems to be a deeper yearning for spiritual awakening and growth nowadays—a profound desire to have a 'more' lived experience, connect with something greater, and achieve a deeper connection to ourselves. Whilst we may often have an end goal in mind in our pursuit of spiritual awakening, this journey is not about reaching a specific destination. But about embracing the present moment's transformative power and using each of those moments to guide us on our part.

We are conditioned since birth (and beyond) to fixate on goals and outcomes as we navigate our path. But true spiritual growth is not about reaching a predetermined endpoint. It is about immersing ourselves in the beauty of each step along the way, relishing the nuances of our experiences, good, bad, or ugly, and finding solace in the present moment because it is in that journey that true transformation resides.

The stories you tell yourself don't need to be your truth.

Our ego is a skilled storyteller and spins tales that shape our perceptions and beliefs. But these stories are not inherently true. They are often coloured by our past experiences, fears, and insecurities and have the power to hold us back from recognising our innate truths and the deeper soul wisdom within our grasp.

Challenge the narratives that hold you back, and question their validity. Do they really speak to the truth of who you are? Reconnect with the vastness of your soul and embrace the power to rewrite your story and see it from a perspective that honours you and aligns with your deepest truth and potential for growth.

You are your soul's temple; honour the privilege.

Within the sanctuary of your physical being, a divine spark resides. You are a vessel of sacred energy, connected to the source of all creation and a vast collective consciousness capable of awe-inspiring growth and self-realisation. Treat your body, mind, and spirit with reverence and care. Nourish yourself with love, kindness, self-compassion and vibrationally aligned food and

experiences. Embrace the privilege of being a custodian of your soul's temple, the body that it chose for this next step in its learning journey. It is within this vessel that your spiritual awakening finds its home. And by finding its home, you will feel at home within the collective energy of humanity.

Breathe into your discomfort and pain; honour it.

Regardless of the path you have travelled, the ebbs and flows of life often bring experiences of discomfort and pain. Instead of shying away from these emotions, lean into them with tenderness and grace. Don't see them as the enemy; breathe deeply and allow yourself to fully experience these sensations, knowing that the potential for growth and healing lies within them and beneath what these emotions may be hiding from you. Honour the lessons they bring and choose to emerge stronger, more resilient, and wiser on the other side.

Acceptance is your soul's natural state.

In the depths of your being, acceptance resides as your soul's natural state. Embrace the totality of your being—

the light and the shadows, the triumphs and the struggles. Allow acceptance for your path and its plights to wash over you like a gentle wave, soothing the resistance and nurturing a deep sense of inner peace. In acceptance, you find liberation and an unwavering connection to your true essence.

Keep your mind and heart open to potential possibilities.

The universe is a vast tapestry of infinite potential and undoubtedly too vast for us to understand intimately and in detail. You can, however, cultivate a mindset of curiosity and openness, allowing yourself to witness the miracles that unfold in your life. When you approach each moment with an open heart and an open mind, you invite the magic of synchronicity and serendipity to weave its way into your existence. It is a way of receiving guidance on your path, so trust in the beauty of the possibilities that show up for you, for they hold the key to your spiritual expansion.

Embrace all experiences; you are perfect regardless.

Whether you want to believe it or now, every experience has its purpose and significance in helping you grow and learn more about yourself and your purpose here. The best gift you can give yourself is to embrace the light and the dark, the joy and the sorrow, the laughter and the tears. Within the mosaic of your experiences, you discover the radiant truth that you are perfect, whole, and complete. Embrace your authenticity, for it is a testament to the divinity that resides within you.

Stop comparing your spiritual growth to others; you are life itself and were born to have your own experience!

In the realm of spiritual awakening, comparison serves no purpose except the ego. Each soul follows a unique path, a sacred dance choreographed by the universe. Release the need to compare your journey to others and honour the wisdom emanating from your unique perspective. You are life itself, experiencing its wonders through your singular lens. Embrace your individuality and find solace in the depth of your own truth.

See the lesson in everything, use them as tools for growth. Choose to reflect and learn from them.

Life is a symphony of lessons, each moment a potential and opportunity for growth. Pause, reflect, and discern the teachings that lie within your experiences. Whether they manifest as blessings or challenges, embrace them as catalysts for your spiritual expansion. Through self-reflection and a willingness to learn, you transform life's lessons into stepping stones towards self-realisation.

The world is your mirror and a reflection of what you energetically project.

As you traverse life, remember that the world around you is a mirror, reflecting your energetic vibrations. Observe the patterns and dynamics that unfold in your interactions, for they are mirrors reflecting aspects of yourself. Take responsibility for the energy you project and cultivate the love, compassion, and authenticity you wish to see reflected in your outer reality.

As you nurture your spiritual evolution and become aware of your profound spiritual awakening and growth journey, hold these teachings close to your heart because they will be a helpful tool to use as you continue to seek your truth. Embrace the beauty of the present moment, honour your experiences, and celebrate all the wisdom life's moments teach you.

You are a seeker choosing to walk the path of self-discovery and expansion. Make the most of every moment. It will illuminate your path and lead you back home to yourself.

Life is a symphony of lessons,
each moment a potential and
opportunity for growth.

YOU CAN
any

DO

thing

From Anxiety and Depression to Living with Purpose

By Kylie Attwell

A Personal Story

KYLIE ATTWELL, THE FOUNDER OF A GUIDE FOR LIFE, SHARES HOW SHE WENT FROM BEING A PEOPLE PLEASER TO HAVING UNSHAKABLE INNER CONFIDENCE AND THE FREEDOM TO EXPRESS HERSELF FULLY.

My mother tells me that even as a tiny baby, I used to projectile vomit the moment I perceived any tension in the room, and for as long as I can remember, I was plagued with a deep sense of melancholy that rarely left me.

To many, being born into a nuclear family and growing up in a small country town sounds idyllic. For me, it was oppressive. My family and school life were emotionally and physically volatile. To avoid an unwarranted spanking with the cane handle of the feather duster, a severe scolding or schoolyard bullying, I became a goody-two-shoes and people pleaser. I lacked all sense of self.

I believed my misery was due to the emotionally and physically volatile environment in which I'd been raised, so in my mid-teens, I hatched an escape plan. As soon as I finished high school, I was moving to the city. My real life would start there. I'd get a part-timejob and go to university with the goal of becoming independent, financially and emotionally.

Having followed through on my plan, by the time I'd reached my late 20s, I had everything that I thought would make me happy: a secure and lucrative career, my dream house, a classic car I loved, a busy social life, designer things, and heaps of 'friends'.

I was supposed to feel happy and fulfilled, right? Except I wasn't. I felt hollow and deeply unhappy. I wondered if there was something fundamentally wrong with me.

This time, I assumed my misery was due to there being no real joy in my life, so I followed my heart and set up a business based on my love for architecture and design. Soon Prince Charming arrived on the scene. Yet, deep down, I still felt empty inside.

Fast forward ten years, the fairy-tale romance had ended, and I'd closed my business. I was freshly divorced and now broke, both emotionally and financially. I felt like a complete failure. What now?

Being a logical person, I went searching for what was 'missing'. I changed careers multiple times — I've been a radiographer, decorative finishes tradie and event manager. When that didn't work, I did what any normal human does and turned to personal development. After spending thousands on books, seminars, workshops, and retreats, I still felt lost and confused about what would make me happy. I hit rock bottom.

After a 16-year self-discovery journey, I finally came across key people (or I could say the Universe sent them) that helped me see what was missing, that is, a sense of purpose. They helped me realise that building a life centred around passion offers temporary satisfaction, but it is not the answer to creating a joyous, fulfilling and meaningful life. It was only through uncovering and embodying my life's calling that I developed a sense of purpose, a reason to live. That's when my life started to change dramatically and quickly, in my early 40s.

Once I'd found and owned my purpose, I started to KonMari my life.

This involved becoming mindful of my thoughts and what I said. I refrained from complaining and re-living situations that made me feel unhappy and frustrated. I learned to focus on 'mentally rehearsing' my ideal day.

Putting my needs first became a priority. I stopped doing things out of guilt and obligation. I no longer said yes to things I didn't want to do just to please others. Instead, I chose to engage in activities that brought me joy and spent time with people who inspired and uplifted me. I also turfed out possessions that didn't spark joy or harboured bad memories.

I dealt with my emotional baggage by learning and applying emotional release techniques such as the Emotional Freedom Technique (aka EFT or Tapping) and the Emotion Code. Learning to generate feelings of gratitude, appreciation and kindness on command also helped me to sustain an elevated emotional baseline throughout my day.

And I worked through clearing my self-limiting beliefs by using a cutting-edge belief-change process known as PSYCH-K. After around six months of implementing these actions, I could think more clearly, and my inner voice began to emerge. As I started to express my needs and desires, my life unfolded with more ease. The more I developed an intimate relationship with myself, the more I began to trust expressing myself fully in the world at large. The 'people pleaser' was now gone.

With hindsight, I didn't need to become someone else to step into my life's purpose: it's who I already was at my very core. This is also a central message of many great spiritual teachers. All I needed to know was where to look and what questions to ask myself. My confidence and sense of fulfilment continued to grow with every new step I took towards embodying my life purpose.

I felt called to share with others the resources that transformed my life — so they could skip the thousands of dollars and 16-year journey. That's when I stepped into my life's purpose and began curating the information and methodologies referenced in my *A Guide for Life* and the *Build a Life You Love Workbook Series*.

Living my life's calling hasn't been an easy journey or without challenges; however, every step of the way has been enjoyable and deeply rewarding. Sure, I get frustrated at times because things don't happen in the way I think they should, in the timeframe I want them to, but I've never once lost my enthusiasm or belief in what I do.

Everything else pales in comparison. It's beyond passion. This mission to help people be an authentic expression of who they are at their core and live with meaning is part of me. It's who I am, and I feel deeply privileged and honoured to do this work. Now that I've discovered and am living my purpose, there is no turning back.

It's this sort of focus and exuberance that makes the impossible possible and has the capacity to create real change in the world. This verve also exists within you and, when unleashed, will alter your experience of life profoundly and irrevocably.

Although you might not realise it, you possess a unique combination of innate abilities, skills and life experiences that allows you to serve others in a way that only you can. In particular, it's the challenges you've overcome that give you the compassion and experience to transform the lives of others.

Kylie Attwell is an author, content curator and self-transformation facilitator. Her services take a multi-disciplinary approach based on the latest therapeutic modalities and brain science. Kylie conducts one-on-one consultations and energy assessments to ascertain where clients are on their journey and then provides personalised guidance to help change the printout of their life.

Visit Kylie's website at www.aguideforlife.com

DIVE
INTO
SPIRIT
SOUL
LOVE
LIFE

Behind the Pages

A 3rd Birthday Retrospective Exploring the Journey
of a Magazine with Founder Kim Bleeze

> *We can throw every excuse at ourselves to not do the thing, but we are only hurting ourselves, and you'll always be left thinking, "What if?" if you don't. The thing about the universe is that it wants us to succeed and is constantly putting opportunities in front of us.*

Fueled by an unwavering desire to create a sacred space where souls can unite and share their passions and life's purpose, Kim Bleeze embarked on an inspiring journey to bring Fierce Truths Magazine into the world. And now, as we celebrate its third birthday, we couldn't think of a better way to honour this milestone than to sit down with our visionary founder herself and dive behind the pages of her creation.

As we plunge into the heart of our conversation, Kim bares her soul, recounting the exhilarating highs, the challenging lows, and the vibrant dreams that dance within her. We'll get a brief glimpse into the fabric of her being, her personal connection to this challenging journey, and the profound impact of birthing such a magnificent beacon of mind, body, and spiritual wisdom into the world.

Together, we'll celebrate the intricate tapestry of growth that both Kim and Fierce Truths Magazine have experienced.

Oh, but let's not forget the wild adventure of transformation that Fierce Truths Magazine has taken over the years! We'll explore the winding path that led the magazine to discover its voice, navigating twists and turns, shedding old layers, and emerging as an award-winning publication of spiritual truth. It is an interview that speaks to Kim's resilience, courage, and unwavering dedication that continues to pour into her heart's mission.

Fierce Truths Magazine is not merely a publication—but a guiding light, illuminating the way to a life lived in harmony with your most profound desires and beliefs.

So, dive headfirst into the wisdom that Kim Bleeze shares, and together, let's celebrate the past, embrace the present, and eagerly anticipate Kim's creations yet to come. Fierce Truths Magazine is more than ink on paper—it's a testament to the power of following your heart's calling and spreading the spiritual truth into the world.

FTMag: Kim, can you share about yourself with our readers who don't know who you are?

Kim: I'm used to asking this question, so being on the receiving end of an interview always feels strange! Before anything, I am a single mum of two incredible adults. I am a down-to-earth woman who loves to travel, walk barefoot on the earth and beat her drum to the morning sun. What many of the readers might not know is that I actually travel full-time and live in my van most of the time. Which people often find super strange.

My first love is spirit and my calling as a medium and teaching people about our soul journey. I am, of course, also the founder of this beautiful magazine, which has been such a gift to birth into the world and now THE SOUL JOURNEY APP. I am also birthing my company's book publishing component, which is still hush-hush. I am so excited about it, though. I could burst!

FTMag: It's three years on? Talk to us about your journey.

Kim: I can't believe it has been three years! Wow, what an experience it has been with many mistakes that have bought many incredible lessons. Put it this way, if I was to choose one word to associate with my journey to birth a magazine into the world, it would be 'Challenge', and it has been, in all the best ways, but also some really difficult ways too.
I totally threw myself into the deep end when I decided to create a magazine, and I had no idea what I was doing. I have to wonder sometimes if I even do now! This journey has pushed and continues to push me from the start.

Three years on, and that hasn't changed. I am just more adapted at navigating it now and getting better (I think!) every day at taking on more of a 'publisher' role within my psyche, which I struggle with. This big part of me wants to lock myself away from the world and spend my days creating art and jewellery. But apparently, and much to my horror, my path and purpose are bigger than that. So I find myself in this constant state of resistance – like a child getting told to do a chore when they'd much rather play!

I laugh at myself every day I recognise this within myself. So I breathe and connect into my heart, which is very connected to my bigger vision, and continue to commit to this journey. Even if some days I am holding on by a thread.

FTMag: You spoke about your future visions when we interviewed you for our 1sr birthday. Has anything changed knowing what you know now?

Kim: My future vision has always been to build a platform to support people sharing their truth. My idea was to go into book publishing eventually, and that hasn't changed as a way of really helping people. Now I have our education app, THE SOUL JOURNEY, as a way of doing that too.

If anything, the vision and what I am creating has just gotten bigger. Enormous from where I am sitting at the moment, in a "how the hell am I going to achieve that' sort of way. And I do not know if I will make it happen, right? I only know one thing; if I don't show up, my vision won't happen at all. I owe it to my path and the people to whom I can give a voice to give it my best shot.

FTMag: What are the highs and lows of becoming a magazine publisher?

Kim: So many, and all possible over a day! Most magazines have big teams for a reason, but with us, it is 80% me, so it often feels like too bigger a job for me - I have come close to quitting so many times.

Yet each time I sit precariously on that fence, something fortifies my path and gives me the courage and inspiration to keep going. For example, I recently had one of those moments and felt I was done. I was even contemplating the steps I'd need to take to close my company down. Then the print issues of the magazine I'd ordered arrived, and I saw how beautiful they looked and felt in my heart how important it is for Fierce Truths Magazine to be out in the world. She has so much change to help bring to our reader's hearts. How could I not want to honour that? So I shook all that shitful thinking away and focused on the incredible gift I am contributing to the world instead and how important she is. Other times have been a PR to a Hollywood actress reaching out to secure an interview. Or Gabby's Bernstein saying yes to an email interview for our last issue.

They both happened when I contemplated the magazine's path and whether or not I should keep going. I took them as confirmation that I should keep going, which is a win.

FTMag: What is the one message you want to say to someone sitting on the sidelines of following their own purpose and unsure if they should take the step?

Kim: Just fucking do it. Say yes to yourself and honour whatever way you are here to contribute to the world. We can throw every excuse at ourselves to not do the thing, but we are only hurting ourselves, and you'll always be left thinking, "What if?" if you don't. The thing about the universe is that it wants us to succeed and is constantly putting opportunities in front of us. That is translated to us through moments of inspiration, and you have a choice to say yes to it in that moment. The opportunity will move on to the next soul if you don't.

I've lost count of the times I've thanked myself for saying yes to being brave enough to birth Fierce Truths Magazine.

We love Our Covers

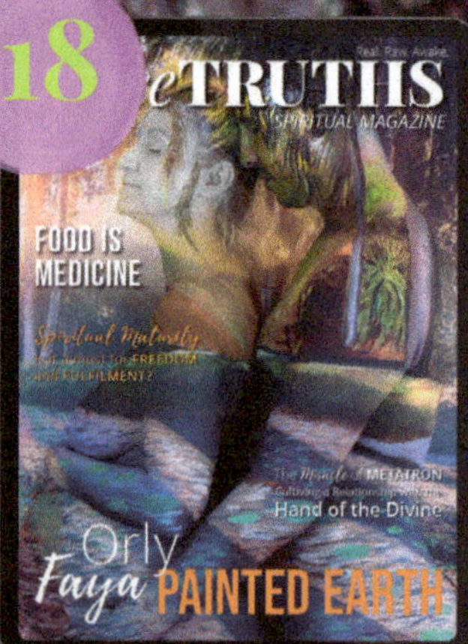

ceTRUTHS
SPIRITUAL MAGAZINE
Larisa Gosla
WE ARE ALL MUSIC

ceTRUTHS
SPIRITUAL MAGAZINE
Easy Guide to Using Tarot Cards
Spirit of LOMI LOMI interview with Dawn Charlton
Peter Williams
JUST LIVE LIFE

ceTRUTHS
SPIRITUAL MAGAZINE
MEET ANGEL ARIEL
HELP HER RAISE THE VIBRATION of HUMANITY

ceTRUTHS
SPIRITUAL MAGAZINE
Fierce TRUTHS Magazine

ceTRUTHS
MAGAZINE
Embrace YOUR NAKEDNESS
OWN YOUR EMOTIONAL Sovereignty
The Most Important Relationship is With YOURSELF
Leela Cosgrove
BADASS AND HIGH PRIESTESS OF HARD TRUTHS speaks
INTUITIVE BUSINESS

ceTRUTHS
MAGAZINE
6 SPIRITUAL HABITS That can help change your life
DEFENSIVENESS
And why interests havoc in your relationship
How to Escape Materialism and live a happier life

ceTRUTHS
MAGAZINE
EMMA HAMLIN
Do you want to be an author of influence?
True Love is not Possessive
Are you jealous?
ALLOW IT TO TRANSFORM YOU
21 Signs your new Positive Mindset

eTRUTHS
MAGAZINE
Be Brave becoming the Leader you were Born to Be
STOP Spiritually Bypassing

ceTRUTHS
MAGAZINE
SACRED GEOMETRY
Breaking THROUGH THE MATRIX
DILLON FORTE

eTRUTHS
MAGAZINE
Gentle Aquarius
MAKE AN IMPACT BE THE CHANGE
Journey of ASCENSION

TRUTHS
MAGAZINE
Capricorn Business Balance and Money Mindset
Nicolle Edwards
RIZEUP

eTRUTHS
MAGAZINE
Erica Lippy
ELEVATORS THE HUMAN SPIRIT
Sagittarius
Personal Truth
Adventurous
Culture
Positive
Independant

eTRUTHS
MAGAZINE
Scorpio Power Rebirth Transformation Expansion
Deva Wild
EMBODIED SENSUALITY
OUR GIFTED GODDESS

ceTRUTHS
MAGAZINE
Are you struggling with your mental health?
Tap into Joy
IS IT TIME TO FIND YOUR TRIBE?
MEET SAM HIGGINS
GIFTED GODDESS

eTRUTHS
MAGAZINE
MEET GIFTED GODDESS COLBY REBEL
What is Your Superpower?
It's time to let go
MEET OUR TEAM

ceTRUTHS
MAGAZINE
The Silent Pain of Domestic Violence
7 WAYS TO EXPRESS YOURSELF
MEET GIFTED GODDESS LISA WILLIAMS
OUR INAUGURAL ISSUE

FTMag: How has the magazine evolved in content and design since its inception?

Kim: I think when you can look back at earlier work and cringe, you know you've grown, haha! I do that with our earliest issues. Not because the content and design weren't great, it was. I might be biased, but I truly believe that every issue we have published has been incredible. Still, it just keeps getting better and better. The articles, not dating them, the design, and especially the covers and the covers have probably been the most significant change we've made. And choosing to publish bi-monthly instead of monthly and making it a 120-pages tabletop magazine that you could read ten years after release and it still be relevant.

At the start, not knowing anything about magazines, I made a lot of assumptions about what I thought they needed to be. One of them assumed that we needed to have our interviewees on the covers, which meant we had to make do with the images they supplied us with. The covers still looked great but didn't speak to who we were as a spiritual-themed magazine. By the end of 2021, the magazine's energy was calling for a change, so I called it, and I think it is the smartest choice I could have made. You only need to look back at our covers to see the difference. Our app has evolved too. We had to change app hosts because the old one had many glitches not addressed as diligently as you would expect from an app software company. Readers have problems accessing the magazine after purchase. So we lost many subscribers, received abuse on social media and had to issue many refunds because of it. Now our app is through a different company, and we haven't looked back.

FTMag: What are some of the highlights and milestones you are most proud of during the magazine's three-year journey?

Kim: Publishing our interview with Gabby Bernstein, whom I admire tremendously, would have to be the biggest. Although it was only an email interview, it still meant a lot. Gabby's work first inspired me to get comfortable sharing my story, ultimately leading to Fierce Truths Magazine's birth.

Another is our print issues; they are beautiful! Especially now that they are 120 pages of spiritual growth goodness! They are only print-by-demand at this stage, but I am focusing a lot more on getting them in stores this year. We are also in over 1000 digital newsstands, bookstores and libraries, which is a huge achievement. We've also just signed another distribution contract, so I can't wait to see what that brings to our reach. Sometimes I google us to get my fix on seeing how much we have grown – we are everywhere! And oh, we won a ROAR LEADERSHIP AWARD!

FTMag: Can you share some behind-the-scenes stories or challenges that you faced while building and running the magazine?

Kim: Me trying to build the whole thing whilst living and travelling full-time in a van would have to be one of the biggest ones! Who actually does that? It's crazy. I had to do an interview once in the toilets of the camping ground I was staying at to get decent internet access. My choice of lifestyle definitely makes it challenging, but would I choose differently? No, I don't think so. I love being on the road. I just need to have a better structure to how I do things and a more lifestyle/work balance so I don't keep burning my candle at both ends. Our budget for marketing is another one. I started the magazine through that first wave of lockdowns while I was in bed with nerve problems in my back in 2020. I didn't have business capital, so we've never had significant expenses for advertising or branding. It makes it challenging to build brand awareness on the scale I would like it to be to the point that I am currently sitting with the idea of bringing in an angel investor to get this party really started.

FTMag: What role does your magazine play in the larger media landscape, and how do you differentiate yourself from other publications?

Kim: As an indie magazine, we are so small scale compared to the larger media landscape. I fluctuate between seeing that as good and detrimental to what I am trying to build. I can't decide! When I do some self-inquiry into that more, though, my fear of being more visible agrees we should stay small. Because the reality of what I want to build is that Fierce Truths Magazine is recognised everywhere and read by soul seekers all over the world. And, of course, we need visibility to do that.

Fierce Truths Magazine has depth. She speaks to your soul and guides you to be a better version of yourself without the fluff and more aligned with your life path in a way that facilitates profound growth and spiritual evolution. Then by the same token, giving you the tools you need to get the best out of your human experience.

FTMag: What are your aspirations and goals for the magazine in the next three years?

Kim: Witnessing each new issue come together. That time of the month is often so wild with everything to do, and I always feel like we won't make the deadline, it won't come together in time, or we won't have enough content. But it does, and she's beautiful – EVERY TIME.

FTMag: How has starting and running this magazine impacted your own personal growth and development?

Kim: This journey is incredible at showing me all the ways I am yet to grow and all the ways I am not walking my talk if I flounder on my path. It is leaving no room for me to stay small (unfortunately!) because I am coming to realise for the magazine to be seen, I need to get comfortable with being seen too, and that is uncomfortable and pushes my edges in ways I'd rather ignore, but I can't. My heart won't let me hold off anymore.

FTMag: What has been the most valuable lesson you've learned as a magazine founder and entrepreneur?

Kim: Stay focused on what you are creating, and keep going. To develop strong boundaries to what you say yes to and what you say no to. That meant learning to say no to anything that does not align with my business and what I am trying to build. That came with me thinking I could do all the things at once, where it needs to be about prioritising my goals and working only from what was important for my company to grow right now.

So every time I have a colleague or friend say, hey, do this thing with me, like an event or show or something, I need to be firm to my commitment and say no. It's been challenging, and I am sure I won't be saying no forever, but I am

for now. I am sure there are other lesson's I could share too, but this has been the one more prominate for me this year.

FTMag: How do you manage the inevitable ups and downs that come with running a magazine, and what keeps you motivated during challenging times?

Kim: Trusting in what will be is a big one. This allows me to let go of what is not working and go with the direction I am getting pulled in, not being scared to change direction if needed.

Actually, let me rephrase that as it is not entirely true – to be willing to change direction even if it scares me, I'm still working on that one!

FTMag: Have there been any sacrifices you've had to make to ensure the magazine's success, and how do you handle the balance between work and personal life?

Kim: My sociability is what suffers the most. Running the magazine and working on our expanding areas is exhausting. Even when I am not working, I still give it mental energy to my vision because I find it challenging to switch off. So at the end of the day, the last thing I feel like doing is getting on the phone. I was never a big phone talker anyway, but now I am considerably worse – haha, just ask my friends! We have to pre-book our catchups because I am so precious with my energy, and so I am constantly mindful to not overload my plate, which I am an epic fail at often. I am learning though.

FTMag: Looking back at the past three years, what advice would you give yourself when starting out as a magazine founder?

Kim: Don't do it!!! Haha only joking, well, sort of! Seriously though, if you feel called to it, go for it, but do your research and be prepared to invest a lot of your time thoroughly. Especially if you want to do it properly. You could follow a few avenues to get it out into the world, find what works for you and stay the course. If your vision is worth it, you'll find the hard work worth it too.

FTMag: Last question. Kim, what is your fierce truth?

Kim: Ooo I LOVE this question! I like to answer it by touching my heart and asking from that space. My answer today is the acknowledgement of how incredible we all are, how incredible I am. Our soul fought to have a place to learn in this world, and we are the ones that made it. My truth right now is that I will treasure this experience and really make the most of answering the call to be more and do more out in the world.

Now, as founder, I get to ask you. What is your fierce truths?

TAKE A

Break

THE ANCIENT WISDOM OF
TREES
EXPLORING SPIRITUAL CONNECTIONS

Amid our busy lives, finding a moment of tranquillity and connection with the world around us can be a fantastic way to bring ourselves back home to self. One of the most extraordinary ways to achieve that is by hanging out with our tree friends! Deep-rooted in Mother Earth and each with its own unique spirit, these majestic beings have witnessed countless cycles of life, weathered storms and stood tall throughout centuries of our history. They can communicate with each other and those of us willing to listen. By tapping into their wisdom and healing vibes, we unlock a new level of deep spiritual connection and heart-opening.

It Starts with *Intent*

First, find a tree that calls out to you, one that resonates with your heart and soul. Or, at the very least, listen for that little nudge or pull of curiosity towards a tree you feel drawn it. Maybe it's an oak tree's sturdy presence or a willow's graceful branches blowing in the wind. Trust your instincts and let yourself be guided to the trees that hold a special connection for you, and once you've found it, approach your tree with genuine respect and awe, acknowledging its inherent wisdom and amazing presence. Give the trunk a gentle touch, feeling the texture and temperature beneath your fingertips. Express gratitude for the tree's existence and extraordinary gifts to humanity.

Presenting a little offering to your tree friend can be super powerful. It doesn't have to be anything fancy —maybe a handful of wildflowers, a heartfelt note, or a tiny crystal. Choose something personally significant to you and offer it with love and gratitude. This gesture symbolizes the beautiful give-and-take relationship we have with the natural world.

Now that you've built rapport get comfy near it. Relax and let go of all the day's tension. Take a few deep breaths, settle yourself in the present moment, and get ready to listen now that you're in the zone!

Trees communicate in the most subtle ways— vibrations, energetic exchanges, silent whispers of thought; you name it. Pay close attention to the sensations and emotions that bubble up within you. Trust your gut and see what insights or messages come your way. It might be a word, an image, a feeling that speaks to you, or simply a sense of presence. Tree talk is two-sided, and they might want to hear from you as much as you do them. So if you're feeling adventurous, you can take the lead and guide the conversation. Hold an intention in your mind or whisper it softly to your chosen tree.

Be open and receptive to the messages and deep wisdom they have to share. Trust your inner compass and allow the tree's wisdom to unfold in its unique way.

Take a moment *to express your heartfelt thanks to the tree for its wisdom, presence, and incredible healing energy.*

Speak your gratitude out loud or silently in your heart. *Let the tree know that you appreciate its role in the grand tapestry of life and the valuable lessons it imparts.*

What Happens When You *Hug* a Tree ?

Simple, it's a transformative and healing experience! Think of it as a VIP ticket to a stronger connection with nature. Using all your senses, you're immersing yourself in the natural world's physical, psychological, and emotional impact.

When you wrap your arms around a tree, your energetic field merges with its own, creating a beautiful energy exchange. This connection helps restore balance and harmony within your being. Trees are like energy superheroes, grounding and cleansing your energy, supporting emotional healing, and nurturing your spiritual growth. Plus, hugging a tree can banish stress, anxiety, and feelings of isolation by giving you that cozy sense of belonging and connection with nature.

Hugging a tree also unlocks a deeper understanding of our relationship with the natural world.

It reminds us that we're not alone; we're part of a vast interconnected web of life, where each living being has a unique contribution to make. Every encounter with a tree nurtures our sense of belonging. It reminds us of the importance of protecting and preserving our precious natural resources.

The spiritual connection with trees is a personal and unique experience for each of us. Every encounter holds the potential for growth, healing, and transformation. So, let your intuition be your guide, and listen closely to the whispers of their infinite wisdom.

And one last thing—tree wisdom isn't limited to forests. Trees are everywhere! You can find them in parks, gardens, and even city streets. So, wherever you are, take a moment to pause, tune in, and connect with a tree. By nurturing this spiritual bond, you'll deepen your relationship with nature and unlock the profound interconnectedness of all life on Earth.

" Spontaneity
is the best kind
of adventure "
- Author unknown

"The spiritual journey is the unlearning of fear and prejudices and the acceptance of love back in our hearts.

Love is the
essential reality
and our purpose
on earth

To be consciously
aware of it, to
experience love in
ourselves and
others, is the
meaning of life."

-Marianne Williamson

Moon Phases

NEW MOON

This is the time of new beginnings. Be open. Spend some time dreaming big.

WAXING CRESCENT

Now is the time to set intentions and send them out to the Universe.

FIRST QUARTER

The moment to take action has arrived. Do not let obstacles stop you in your tracks.

WAXING GIBBOUS

Your intentional actions are gaining momentum in this phase. Make sure you stay in alignment.

FULL MOON

A time to reap the reward of your hard work. Be sure to practice gratitude during this time.

WANING GIBBOUS

Start integrating the new lessons you've learned and the experiences you've had. Time to go inward and reflect.

LAST QUARTER

Release and let go the things that no longer serve you by setting the intent to do so.

WAXING CRESCENT

A time for rest and restoration. Take time away from the busyness of your schedule.

THE MOST IMPORTANT *Journey* OF ALL

By Jackie Norman

At the age of 50, I am well accustomed to 'not fitting into anyone's boxes'. In 2016 I sold my house and everything in it and set off for a full-time life on the road, cramming myself, a large, hairy Welshman and an elderly spaniel into a 4.6-metre-long converted builder's van. We had no real plan except to keep travelling and see where we ended up. As a writer and blogger of many years, my loyal readers were also caught up in the excitement and romance of it all. What my now-husband Gareth and I didn't know, however, was that my previously fit and healthy body was about to fall apart in ways we could never have begun to imagine.

In the five years which followed, I lived with crippling endometriosis and adenomyosis (which resulted in a full hysterectomy), chronic pain, vulvodynia, fibromyalgia and IBS, all while supposedly 'living the dream' in our tiny house on wheels. When Covid forced us to end our travels and return to conventional life in 2021, things went from bad to worse, and I was spending most of the time bedridden in agony, feeling as though my body was being pulled limb from limb. By June of 2022, my life 24/7 was laying immobile on a mattress on the lounge floor. My skin felt like it was on fire, the pain was unbearable, and the medical professionals gently told me there was nothing more they could do for me.

I felt as though my body hated me, that it was constantly attacking me, and I couldn't understand why this was happening to me and not everyone else. I came to believe that I deserved it. I deserved it because I was a bad person who must have done something terrible in a past life, and this was my punishment. I was suicidal and truly believed it would be better for both myself and Gareth if I simply wasn't here any more.

I could see that my state of mind was destroying Gareth, however, and couldn't bear to think how much I was hurting him, so one day, I dragged myself up off the floor, told myself that the pain was all in my head and that I was going to be 'normal', for his sake. I discovered Wim Hof and cold water therapy, and this, along with EFT and the sheer power of my mind, brought me back from the brink in September 2022. Around this time, my landlady invited us to what she called the 'Peace Education Program', a 10-week free course she was about to start in our village. It was an initiative by Prem Rawat, a spiritual leader she had followed and learned from for over 40 years. At 70 years old, she was and still is the most vibrant and positive person we had ever met, so we figured she had to be doing something right! Despite the fact that I still couldn't even sit on a chair due to the pain and that we didn't want to venture out of the house to see or talk to anyone, we dragged ourselves along, if only to support her.

That evening changed my entire life. It changed my perspective, gave me hope and made me see that life was still very much worth living, and I had better hurry up and make the most of it! I attended every one of those sessions and still listen to his teachings every day.

The same doctor who had informed me the medical profession couldn't help me kindly recommended a homeopath. My very first consult with her enabled her to see the big picture. I didn't have a whole bunch of conditions, but one. A condition that was behind them all – trauma. She referred me to a trauma specialist, and I was diagnosed finally and joyfully with PTSD. Yes, I was joyful because at last, I knew what was wrong with me – and that it wasn't my fault. As the months of therapy went on, I was amazed to find that far from the idyllic, 'perfect' childhood I believed I'd had, I

had actually completely blocked out the first 11 years of my life. Add in an emotionally and sexually abusive marriage as an adult, the death of my first newborn son and family mental illness and suicide... for decades, my body had been keeping tally of the impact of all these and more. Now it was screaming at me to wake up and take notice.

As we neared the end of 2022, by pure coincidence, I came across an ad on Instagram announcing a 21-day Manifesting Challenge by someone called Gabby Bernstein. I rarely used social media, avoided the news where possible, and never watched TV, so I had never heard of her, but something about it jumped out at me. I decided to give it a go. I'll be honest, I had always chuckled at the concept of manifesting and really didn't expect it to work, but I looked at it as a good way to start the New Year and something to focus on. I could not BELIEVE the things which started unfolding in my life about ten days into the Challenge! I had felt unfulfilled in my remote working job for a while but was at a loss to know how to change that or what else I could do. Imagine my amazement when my therapist told me in no uncertain terms that if I wanted any hope of healing, I needed to quit my job - now - and focus entirely for at least a year on therapy and processing the trauma. At first, I thought I couldn't do it - not just physically but financially - I mean, who can?! The fear of being unable to manage meant that I quit my job once and then returned two weeks later before finally admitting that my therapist was right. Somehow, we would make it work. I quit for the last time and never looked back.

Even so, I found it hard to get into the practice of resting and focusing on self-care. At first, I resisted it with a passion, but by now, I was a fully-fledged Gabby Bernstein devotee. Like me, she had also lost her first child, and I knew from the way she spoke that this woman was for real. One spiritual teacher led to another and another, and I came to embrace a whole new way of being, one filled with optimism, gratitude, hope and, most of all, understanding. The more I learned, in particular, about trauma and the different ways it holds us hostage – whether we even realise we are holding on to it or not – made me realise how incredibly fortunate I was to have such a huge toolbox of knowledge and support for my self-care. I was beyond grateful – and sad, for the countless people who are suffering without that help.

As Prem Rawat would say, 'knowledge has no use unless it is shared', so I made it my mission to share that knowledge to help others.

Whether they are walking the same path as me or just need positivity to take into their day, I have plenty to shower upon everyone! Not just me but my husband, Gareth. As I progressed through therapy, it also reawakened his own repressed trauma, and we have been going through our separate healing journeys together. It is a journey we never imagined we would be undertaking, but we can say without a doubt the path to knowing and loving yourself is the most important journey anyone can take.

As experienced podcast hosts in our previous jobs, we were inspired to start our own podcast, 'Finding Your Marbles', as a labour of love with the sole purpose of helping others. It's a podcast dedicated to empowering and equipping people with the ability to overcome life's challenges by sharing our extensive experience of living with trauma, chronic illness and life's infinite uncertainties. We also have great pleasure in bringing listeners some amazing guests, including the doctors, teachers and other inspirational personalities that have helped us to 'find our marbles'.

ALL THE

abundance

YOU DESIRE, EXISTS

WITHIN YOU

I'm all about tribe – unabashedly – and I have a number of them too. For starters, I'm a sober woman, a practicing witch and a dyed-in-the-wool Richmond supporter. I'm also fortunate to have family and pals I love dearly. All of these connections make my life rich, and bring me meaning and purpose.

However, I haven't always felt this tapped in. Towards the end of my drinking I was as isolated AF. I was bored to bits and my life extended no further than work and the local. No wonder I was lonely – it's difficult to commit to doing anything when you're permanently hungover.

Since pulling the pin on drink watched my life unfold in wa have anticipated, but in almo developments, there's been community.

Undoubtedly, while we're in a pandemic, there are some limitations on how we can b but it's not impossible. I kno experience, feeling isolated favours, so, right now, I hav harder. With that in mind, I primo suggestions for find and getting connected.

SPIRITUALITY, HEALING, AND HOPE

A Personal Journey to Overcoming Ulcerative Colitis

By Farita Khambatta

My name is Farita, and I am a living testament to the power of the mind, body, and spirit in achieving health and wellness. My story is one of hope, courage, and perseverance in the face of a debilitating autoimmune condition called ulcerative colitis.

In 2001, I was diagnosed with this chronic inflammatory disease that affects the large intestine. The symptoms were excruciatingly painful, bloody, mucus-filled stools that left me feeling helpless and hopeless. Ulcerative colitis made me feel like life was not worth living. I constantly struggled with intense fear and anxiety over leaving the house or being too far from a bathroom.

Over the years, I underwent multiple hospitalisations and prescription medications that provided temporary relief but failed to address the root cause of my illness. It was not until June 2021, when my doctor informed me that my colon was so scarred from years of flares that surgery was my only option, that I knew I needed to take control of my health and life.

Despite the doctor's prognosis and 70% chance of cancer, I refused to accept surgery as my fate.

I turned to natural healing methods, a new mindset, and a deep connection to my spirituality to heal my body from within.

The first step in my journey to wellness was to shift my mindset from victim to victor. I realised that I had allowed myself to be consumed by fear and negativity for too long, and I had the choice to take back control of my life and find joy again. I began to learn the wonders of the mind-body connection with great spiritual thought leaders like Dr Joe Dispenza, Gregg Braden, and Bruce Lipton and the power of Rapid Transformational Therapy (RTT) developed by Marisa Peer.

RTT helped me identify and release limiting beliefs and negative self-talk holding me back from true healing. I learned to tap into my inner strength and resilience and trust in my body's wisdom to heal itself. I would often mentally picture my colon as perfect, pink and healthy and with the help of RTT, I began to shift my focus from illness to wellness and see myself as healthy and vibrant.

Next, I modified my diet to support my healing journey. I researched the latest findings on gut health, autoimmune diseases, and nutrition and discovered the power of a plant-based, anti-inflammatory diet. I added supplements like probiotics, turmeric, vitamin D and omega-3s to support my gut health and reduce inflammation.

I also turned to meditation, yoga, prayer and other mindfulness practices to reduce stress, promote relaxation and keep me focused on my wellness. I connected with nature and found solace in spending time outdoors and practising gratitude for the blessings in my life.

Six months after my diagnosis, I returned to the doctor for a follow-up colonoscopy, and the results were miraculous. The doctor was able to perform the procedure without issue, and my colon appeared healthy and free from scarring. I was elated and felt renewed hope and purpose in my life.

From being bedridden and hopeless, I am now a qualified RTT practitioner, food and wellness blogger, and business owner. I feel blessed to inspire others suffering from chronic illnesses to embrace their power and innate ability to heal themselves.

Farita Khambatta is an RTT practitioner, business owner, wellness blogger, and author. Overcoming years of debilitating physical and emotional damage from inflammatory bowel disease, she rebuilt her life and is now helping others do the same. Farita is passionate about helping others discover and understand their innate power to improve and transform their lives.

Visit Farita at www.linkedin.com/in/faritak

Through my journey, I have learned that healing is not just about the physical body, but it is also a spiritual and emotional journey. It is about shifting our mindset from fear to faith, victim to victor, and illness to wellness. It is about connecting with our inner wisdom, trusting in the power of our body, and tapping into the healing energy of the universe.

Spirituality has played a vital role in my healing journey, and I believe it is a critical component of overall wellness. It is about connecting with a higher power and trusting in the divine plan for our lives.

Finding my power inspired me so much that I am currently in the process of writing a book on everything I learned about this experience so that others who are suffering can be empowered to find their health and healing too.

reminder

vibes don't lie

THE SOUL JOURNEY

DIVE IN

ANYTIME. ANYWHERE

- ✓ BASIC MEMBERSHIP
- ✓ PREMIUM MEMBERSHIP
- ✓ SPIRITUAL TEACHINGS
- ✓ MEDITATIONS
- ✓ MASTERCLASSES
- ✓ COURSES & PROGRAMS
- ✓ EXCLUSIVE ARTICLES
- ✓ COMMUNITY CHAT

THE SOUL JOURNEY

Are you ready for a transformational journey that will help you connect with your soul on a deeper level?

Look no further than THE SOUL JOURNEY.

BE the first to join us and dive into our pre-release content.

Yourself

Self Love Questions

Do I feel guilty if I put my need first?

How important is my own happiness?

In what ways do I show love for myself?

Self Love Journey

I feel loved when:

I feel confident when:

I feel proud when:

I feel blessed when:

Productive Activities:

-
-
-
-
-

Things I'm Grateful for:

Self Improvement

Habits To Change

New Skills To Learn

Values To Enhance

Self Reflection

Monthly Focus

What is my priority for this month?

How can I improve my confidence?

Things I should keep on doing

Things I should stop doing

Vision Board

Wealth Goal	Health Goal

Social	Love	Family

Career	Spiritual	Knowledge

Notes

What else?

Fierce Conversations Podcast

STREAMING NOW

FIERCETRUTHSMAGAZINE.COM/LISTEN-PODCAST

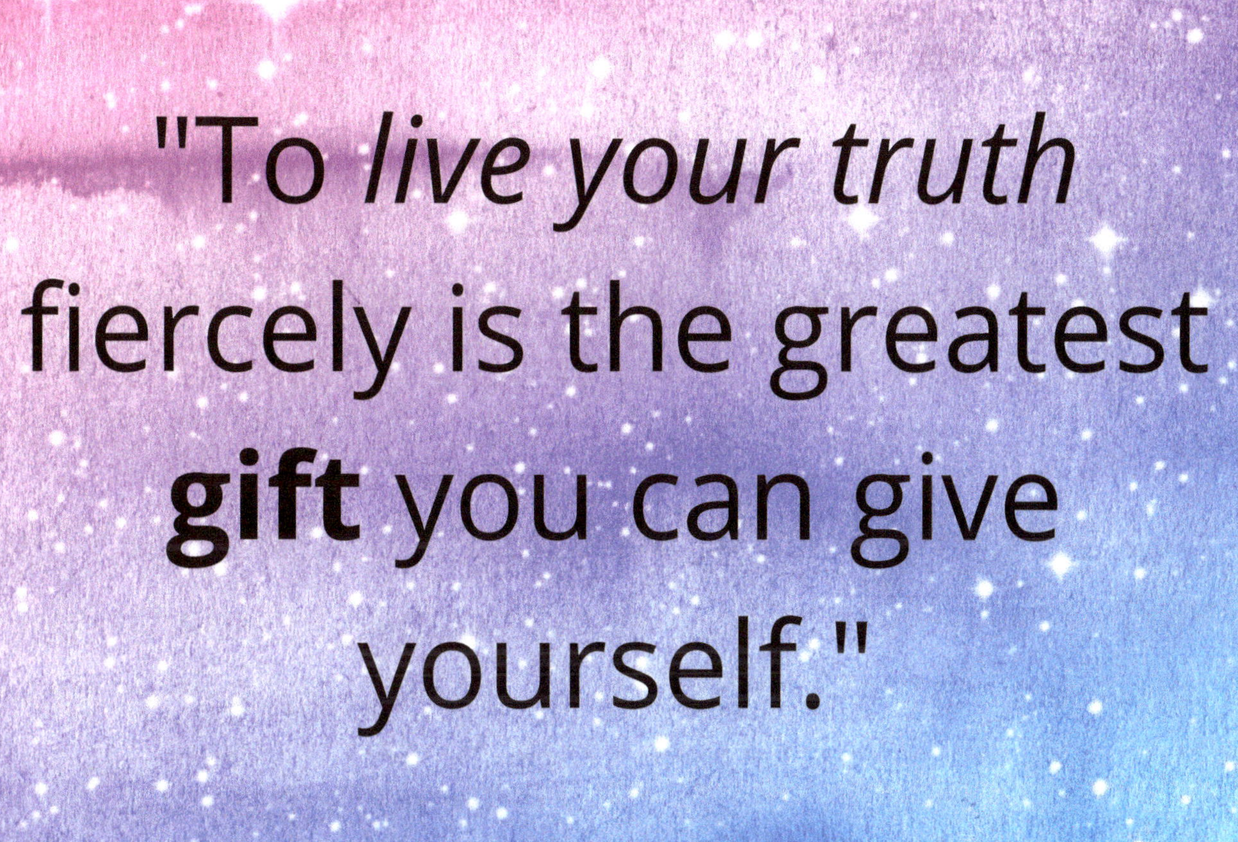

"To *live your truth* fiercely is the greatest **gift** you can give yourself."

- Kim Bleeze
Founder, *Fierce Truths Magazine*

Musings

REGULAR ADVICE AND GUIDANCE FROM
OUR *FIERCE TEAM* OF LIGHTWORKERS

Empowered Healing

Karina Barca

...is a medium, healer, psychic, reiki master, teacher, mentor and forensic healing practitioner. Her passion is to serve, inspire and assist all who want to grow, heal and evolve.

Spirit and Soul

Tui Te Kiri

...is an internationally recognised psychic medium and founder of Our Rising Academy. She's helped 15k+ clients and supports spiritual entrepreneurs to thrive.'

Self Love and WOO

Jasmine Gatt

...is an Intuitive Self Love Coach, Reiki master, psychic intuitive, hypnosis, NLP & ECT practitioner, on mission to guide you to create a loving relationship with yourself.

Channeling a New Earth

Paul Quinton

...is a gifted Spirit Channel and grew up in a psychic family involved in the esoteric all his life. Contributing to Paul fulfilling his soul's contract as a healer, teacher, channel and writer.

Sacred Self Expression

Narelle Clyde

...is a Spiritual Mentor, Retreat Facilitator and #1 Bestselling Author with a passion for guiding others around the globe back to their most authentic self.

Movement Matters

Leila Verban

...is a creative, writer and a qualified Yoga teacher who continues to evolve and refine her skills in counselling, meditation, energy healing and positive manifestation.

The Science of Spirituality

Melanie Oborne

...is a psychologist and researcher who has a passion for bringing together clinical practices, scientific research, and spiritual paradigms to enhance individual's wellbeing.

The Goodness in Grief

Bec Campbell

...is a Medium, Funeral Director and Author. With over thirty years working with spirit, Bec now uses her extensive skill set to help others heal from Grief.

Next Regular Column

Fierce Expert

...imagine writing for an award-winning magazine. Having a chance to share your voice and message with the world.

www.fiercetruthsmagazine.com/ourteam

EMPOWERED HEALING

By Karina Barca

ENERGY

Everything is energy. Everything in this world has an energetic vibration. This includes people, jewellery, clothing, furniture, crystals, houses, buildings, toys, etcetera.

Think about buildings and places where historical events have occurred. You can feel and sense the energy of those times. It may be happy, sad, dense, heavy, spiritual, peaceful, etc.

All the other items mentioned above are the same. So, imagine how much your energy can be impacted daily! Think about the age you are now, all your interactions and all your experiences… that is a lot of energy!

Both good and unpleasant events affect our lives. This transfers as positive and negative energy. The positive energy feeds and nurtures your soul, raising your vibration and life force energy. The negative energy lowers your vibration and may leave you feeling depleted like you are sometimes running on empty.

So, picture, if you will, your daily routine. From the moment you wake up until the time you go to bed. Think about all the things that directly and indirectly affect you emotionally and physically, kids, partner, work, people, trauma, interactions, music etc..

Energy, like you, has no beginning and no end. It can never be destroyed.

It is only ever shifting states.

-Panache Desai

Now imagine beginning that day feeling good, happy, and with positive high vibrational energy. Now imagine feeling tired, cranky and a negative, and low vibration. Which version of you do you think will feel better at the end of the day?

Other everyday events that can affect your energy are going into a store or trying on clothing that someone else has tried on, shopping centres, buying a secondhand piece of furniture, wearing someone else's jewellery, being in someone else's car, house etc. Why? Because energy transfers.

Energy affects everybody. The difference between all individuals that can make a difference is the awareness they have of energy, their spiritual growth and evolution in consciousness.

This information is not to make you feel fear or paranoid. It is simply to bring awareness to the energetic beings that we are and how energy works. Most of the time, you can go about your day without being too affected, but if you are, you now have a better understanding as to why.

If you are sensitive to energy or an empath, you will feel the effects more than others.

So, what can you do about it? First and foremost, awareness is key. Be aware of how you feel, your mood and your energy levels before you venture out, whether it be work, shopping, visiting a friend, a restaurant etc. If your mood or energy changes abruptly or for no apparent reason, it may be highly likely that something, someplace, or someone, has shifted your energy somehow.

You must also remember that all your issues and traumas are energetically carried in your auric field and create stagnant energy or blocks and behaviours which are not in your highest good. This will impact your energetic frequency and be present all the time. Even when you are feeling good, it will run in the background, using your life force energy and can pop up randomly if not dealt with.

Healing is one of the most effective ways in which to shift and clear that energy. Healing sessions deal with the issues whilst also clearing all other energy that may be in and attached to your auric field. It creates a more energetic flow and space for the integration of new awareness, lessons, and growth for your highest good.

Other ways to shift, cleanse and clear your aura and your home and car from time to time are to;

- *Listen to music.*
- *Dance or sing.*
- *Take a bath or swim in the ocean.*
- *Use Sage/Palo Santo to cleanse you, your home, and car.*
- *Ring a bell around you and your home.*
- *Burn incense.*
- *Ground yourself.*

Whether you are at the beginning of your journey or years/decades deep into it, you most likely have experienced life as an emotional roller coaster from time to time. Sometimes due to your own stuff, people's energy around you or the collective energy.

As a healer and psychic medium, I sometimes need to remind myself that not all I am feeling is mine. Although the awareness is there, I can get caught up in life and the emotions I experience in situations and interactions just like anybody else. Many times, it is my own, and many times, it is not mine, but feeling and experiencing it like it is mine. Being sensitive to energy can make it hard to distinguish what is mine and what is not.

I have had to learn through repeated experiences to discern which is which. For example, when I have a client, ninety-nine percent of the time, I will find that my mood may shift abruptly and behave or think like them. Sometimes even dressing or choosing particular colours or jewellery that they love!

I used to think my energy was off or things were just a coincidence, but I could not ignore it when I observed the same behaviours in my clients when they walked in! I now know that is how I work and that it is an insight into what may need to be discussed and/or healed, as the feelings and behaviours are always extremely specific.

The same can also happen with Spirit energy. When they merge with my energy, I will experience the emotions and physical pain they experienced on this earth plane. Although I have my boundaries with Spirit, it can be tricky to discern if it is my own experience when they pop in unexpectedly.

Energetic healing sessions have been one of the most prominent sources of clearing and shifting my energy and maintaining it in flow for me to be a pure and clear conduit and connection to Universal life force energy.

Energetic awareness and growth will always bring what needs to be healed to the surface. It is an empowered way and choice to have clear-flowing energy and to expand and grow in your personal and professional life.

Love, light and blessings,
Karina xx

MOVEMENT
Matters

By Leila Verban

Connecting to mindful muscle activation – how to move with purpose.

By definition, movement is either an act of moving or a change or development. Let's combine both and kickstart this space with ways to make every movement count for your mind and body. Be sure to seek advice from your healthcare provider or fully qualified trainer before attempting any new physical activities.

As a practising yoga teacher that holds multiple classes each week, I have always found my daily mobility and movement to be flexible and fluid.

I recently experienced an injury that I acquired through a fencing accident on the farm, which is a whole other dimension of my life. This accident resulted in bruising to the rear of my ribcage and from impact to my back, also bruising to the cartilage and soft tissues joining to my sternum on the dominant side of my body. For a week, I was barely able to breathe or move my right arm, making movement and relaxing a painful affair!

When faced with injury, the body needs time to rest, to heal and recover. Movement is not always recommended, especially if there are fractures to your bones and damage to the connective tissues or ligaments. After this time of rest, however, there is a transition period when one's body is not only in pain due to the bruising and breaks but also from the tension built up in the body due to mobility being restricted. The muscles begin to seize up, and tension builds in the surrounding muscles and joints connected to those that are injured. With guidance from your doctor or physiotherapist, it's time to start incorporating movement that helps with your recovery. We must retrain the body to function and avoid atrophy.

I started to feel an intense need to stretch my body, however, the pain of stretching meant taking it slow with soft stretches to begin with and following it up with time for rest and recovery. I was fortunate that by 1.5 weeks post-accident, I was holding a small class and decided it was time to start adding more movement to my stretches. I listened intently to what my body was telling me with each pose, and I noticed that there was a threshold between the pain from the injury and the pain from having stepped away from a regular yoga practice. Crazy, it had only been a short time! I needed to connect to my breath, inhaling deep (very slowly) and using my exhales to let go of the tension that had started to create more discomfort for me. When my body told me I had had enough, I found a comfortable position to rest as I continued to guide the class. This was not a time to push me to succeed but grounding myself and listening to what I physically and mentally needed in that moment.

The soft movements I began with are the same movements that benefit us after we wake from a long night of slumber.

In a comfortable seated position, start with:

- Slow rotations of the neck, tying movement to breath.
- A gentle twist to the spine in both directions.
- Slow 'hoola hooping' of the core while seated.
- Side stretches to lengthen the abdominal muscles.

I was unable on the first day to bear my body's weight, so I found ways to accomplish different stretches that may require doing so. This is where the 'hoola hoop' movement while seated is so beneficial for those that have shoulder, arm or wrist injuries. It can be used in place of the 'Cat and Cow' spinal movement performed on all fours. It is also a great idea to utilise props such as a chair, blocks or cushions to bring the ground to you and to soften the pressure on the area of your body that is bearing the weight.

What I love about Yoga as a movement is the diversity in each Asana (pose) and how the practice can be used for recovery after injury or as an ongoing therapy to manage physical pain and mental health. After the first class, in which I was able to perform one-quarter of the movements I was guiding my students through, I found the pain in my body to have lessened significantly, and by the next day, I was able to perform double the amount. It's not a competition and comes down to listening to your body and using Yoga as a tool to connect with your internal world and your physical body. The other aspect of Yoga which is so beneficial for recovery is breathwork.

At significant times in my life, I clearly recall my breath at that moment, from childbirth to panic attacks, to the impact on my body causing extreme adrenalin, to managing pain through movement post-injury and into injury rehabilitation. Yoga offers a practice that connects you to your breath, drawing it deep into your lungs and away from your shoulders. When the body experiences deep abdominal breathing that encourages full oxygen exchange, it can slow the heart rate and reduce blood pressure. Deep breathing calms the nervous system, reduces stress, anxiety and can help relieve pain.

I honestly can thank Yoga and the breathwork within that practice for the strength and support I've needed to persevere through all the trials, tribulations and crazy experiences that life throws my way. I hope this inspires you to give it a go.

SPIRIT & Soul

By Tui Te Kiri

Life is a profound journey of decisions, ranging from mundane daily choices to significant life-changing moments. These decisions are guided by multiple voices within us: our ego, intuition, and the often overlooked but critically important, our Soul and spirit. Mastering the interplay between these inner voices can open doors to profound spiritual growth and success.

At the core of our being lies the Soul, our divine essence, the very spark that connects us to the Universe. It is eternal, resilient, and constantly seeking growth and evolution. Our spirit, on the other hand, is the active expression of our Soul. It carries our life force and is the medium through which our Soul experiences the world.

Alongside our Soul and spirit, we have the ego and intuition, two contrasting yet essential components of our psyche. The ego, formed from years of conditioning, encourages us to stick with familiar, safe, and predictable patterns, much like an overprotective friend. Intuition is the Soul's language, a gentle nudge propelling us towards exploration, growth, and new experiences, even in the face of uncertainty.

The ego, born from the primitive 'fight or flight response of our ancestors, is a self-protection mechanism. It often presents obstacles when we contemplate significant changes, like a career move or a new venture, by highlighting potential risks and failures based on past fears and misconceptions. Deciphering between the ego and intuition can be challenging, but understanding their motivations can provide clarity. The ego's goal is self-preservation, while intuition, the language of the Soul, guides us towards growth and progress. Fear and resistance are often signs of the ego reacting to the call of intuition.

Intuition, the divine whisper of the Soul, is a powerful tool for decision-making. Research in Psychological Science shows that people make more confident and accurate decisions when guided by intuition. Success stories from entrepreneurs and innovators often highlight the role intuition played in their journeys, despite the ego's resistance.

Understanding the ego's role in survival and self-preservation allows us to validate its fears, recognise them as protective mechanisms, and consciously choose to heed the Soul's voice. The Soul, spirit, ego, and intuition are not adversaries but companions on our spiritual journey. Each has a role and serves a different purpose, contributing to our growth and evolution.

Developing trust in your intuition is a gradual process. It begins by observing the subtle signals your intuition sends. Do you experience it as a gut feeling, an inner voice, or an inexplicable knowing? Begin acting on these nudges in small ways and notice the outcomes. This practice will strengthen your bond with your intuition and Soul.

Walking the path of spiritual growth involves recognising your ego's fears, appreciating its intent to protect, yet choosing to listen to your Soul's wisdom, relayed through intuition. As we align our ego with our Soul's longing for growth, we pave the way for spiritual expansion and personal evolution.

Thus, we live and thrive, embodying the highest expressions of our Soul and spirit.

To deepen your understanding and foster this inner harmony, try to reflect on a recent decision you made. Write down your thought process. Did you encounter resistance or fear, signalling the influence of the ego? Or did you sense an inexplicable pull, indicating your intuition speaking? Journaling can provide insights into the interplay of these inner voices in your decision-making process.

Furthermore, rely on your intuition for minor daily choices, such as selecting your attire or planning your meals. By calming your mind and asking inwardly about your genuine desire, you start tuning into your instinctive response, building trust in your intuition.

Also, consider engaging in a simple guided meditation to strengthen your bond with your Soul and intuition. This practice might include focusing on your breath, visualising an inner light, and seeking guidance from the depths of your Soul.

To better appreciate the influence of the ego, try to identify situations where it tends to surface. Is it at work, in personal relationships, or when faced with change? Document the fears or objections your ego raises, and analyse if they are rooted in past experiences rather than the present reality.

Finally, remember the power of words. Adopt daily affirmations to reinforce your faith in your intuition. Use phrases like "I trust my inner guidance" or "My intuition guides me towards the right choices." Regularly affirming these thoughts can help rewire your thoughts, fostering a positive mindset.

By actively engaging in these practices, you can enhance your understanding of your ego, intuition, Soul, and spirit. This inner exploration paves the way for spiritual expansion and personal evolution, enabling you to thrive and embody your Soul's highest purpose. The journey to trusting your intuition involves self-discovery and growth, leading you towards spiritual and personal success.

CHANNELING
A NEW EARTH

The Shadow

By Paul Quinton

It's time to acknowledge what you believe you do not like about yourselves as individual souls. There is a grand opportunity for all humans in this time of upheaval to shift lifetimes of trauma and unresolved emotional charge. What appears to be chaos on your planet is a realignment of consciousness. The universe, including Earth, can seem disorganised, but we assure you all chaos is organised. We want all human beings to see it as such because when you get pulled into the fear, you lower your vibration, which further enhances cellular division, and when your cells are divided, you cannot ground truth and live from that foundation.

The tides are turning within the collective here on Earth. Becoming sovereign beings of your domain is the grandest desire for all planetary consciousness. Humanity is now at the choice of reintegrating with their soul body consciously. The Soul body alignment is the first step to awakening the human experience.

The explosion of plastic surgery comes at a time when humans are required to follow an inward life, and we

Images Credit: Adobe.com/Tryfonov

have seen a rise in the breakdown of self-care and self-love. It is indicative of human projection going the wrong way. Living longer, looking healthier, and overall youth is a progression of light consciousness because as you move closer to the new earth frequency, you live longer, stay younger longer, and use light as nourishment. But what has happened, like most things on your planet, is this energy, the principal fact, has been used oppositely.

You know deep in your soul that this is where you are heading. However, spiritual integrity is so low on the planet that the energy manifests through inadequacy instead of self-love.

In truth, you are living the new earth frequency in its infancy. An example is time; linear time is no longer evident on the planet; it is simply a projection now. That is why three days now feel like the old week, pre-time release. So, you are living in principle in the new Earth, but through 3D reality and 3D reality in your world is an outward projection, not an inward acknowledgement. And this exact situation is occurring on the planet now. You seek to preserve your life through government advice, the vaccine program, and constantly putting foreign materials into your bodies because you believe they will protect you. And from a plastic surgery perspective, it makes you feel better, feel more attractive.

Your consciousness has been manipulated and twisted, making it hard for the average citizen to find any sense in the narrative. When you cut open the body, you run the risk of entity attachment, foreign parasites and bacterial energies from the astral plane. You are giving your power away to not only your ego but also that of the surgeons. Now, like all modern medicine, it has its place and positively serves in numerous ways; however, the intention was to balance between new and old and not to take over all-natural healing and alternative medicine. Still, unfortunately, you give your power away to Doctors, which has been one of the grandest mistakes in collective human consciousness. There is a lot of manipulation by outside sources that infiltrates the medical profession, which is a huge problem.

Now some will say, what about corrective surgery? And we say yes, that's fine because it's all part of your experience in 3D. For example, someone has an accident and needs plastic surgery to realign their face. But because most of humanity lives outwardly, you don't question why you had the accident. Questioning has to be at the forefront. It will soothe the fear and bring a sense of humility as you journey through the human experience of being separate from your universal self. Ask the question first before you go to the surgeon.

What needs to happen in this situation is to realise that for such a grand accident to occur, there must be some serious issues or trauma that hasn't been acknowledged or denied. So, the only way to get their human extension to realise this is for the soul to create a physical manifestation such as an accident. So you see, everything has its place no matter how negative your human mind perceives it to be, but inquisitiveness is lacking in human consciousness. Instead, its action, reaction, and the cycle continues.

When you place foreign materials into your body, you tell your cells you believe you are not already perfect. So, the consciousness within the cells starts to diminish, making it

harder to connect to the soul body because you have lowered the frequency in your DNA. Not to mention that the products they use aren't healthy for your body, even though they say they are fine.

Understand that the medical world is a business first, generating a lot of money, so it magnetises corruption. It is the profound inadequacy in humans that needs dire attention. Inadequacy breeds comparison, and you should never compare yourself with anyone else through 3D reality because, in truth, you are all unique. You are all equal universal beings eternal; there lies true equality.

But if you compare yourself to others through inadequacy, you are more likely to disempower yourself; however, if you compare yourself to another through the soul's eyes, then there would be no judgment because you will see you are all the same. Again, outward projection breeds disempowerment, whereas inward projection breeds enlightenment.

If you have metal plates in your body, metal hips or any foreign material, then you need to send it love every day and change the frequency around the object so it doesn't continue to lower your frequency. If you remember the art of energetic manipulation, you could heal these aspects of yourself without opening the body - you will come back to this in time. But for now, work on your inadequacy and be conscious of your judgments and comparisons.

iMAGE © AikaMozaika / Adobe Stock

SELF LOVE & WOO

Embracing your most creative self and embodying self-expression

By Jasmine Gatt

Whether it comes naturally to you or feels like a bit of a chore, believe it or not, we can all be creative and embrace self-expression. Creativity and self-expression are unique to each individual; there is no one size fits all approach. The good news is, if you don't believe that you are one to express yourself freely and share your creative magic- you just haven't found your own way yet.

Firstly, let's circle back to why it is important to embrace our inner creativity. Let's think of our own energy source for a moment, constantly moving and flowing through us. At times, we may feel stuck, uncertain and unable to see the direction ahead, feeling out of place. By involving ourselves in creative practices, we encourage the flow of energy, moving through stagnant energy. We allow ourselves to connect with our true selves and understand our current emotional and spiritual state. A creative practice that you connect with gives you a physical representation of your internal state. You can channel your energy into something that you can physically see coming to life.

What are some different ways to be creative? It is important to note the significance of finding a practice that resonates with and feels good for you personally- this is absolutely essential. Forcing yourself to invest your time into things that aren't in alignment with you and your direction pushes you further away from connection with self.

When it comes to experimenting with these practices, you may read or hear of something that has been profound for one person, yet when you try it yourself, you don't have the same impactful experience. What is golden for one individual doesn't guarantee that you will enjoy the same results. Allow yourself to be free and experiment with different creative methods to find your own fit. You, your interests, hobbies and joys are all unique; how wonderful you can build and create a creation and self-expression outlet that mirrors your individuality.

You may have had a creative practice in the past that you have since lost touch with. It is normal (and exciting) because we naturally change, grow and evolve, and with that, our interests and practices do the same.

Try not to be disheartened if your once love of dance just isn't scratching your creative itch anymore. It is a wonderful opportunity to play and experiment with what you love. True joy in life is to flow; how wonderful it can feel to move and progress.

Self-expression can be intimate if you want it to be, that is. It can also be a beautiful, fluid outward practice. When we express ourselves, we feel more connected to ourselves and our emotions, and we can outwardly articulate our internal state of being. How magical!

The profound value of self-expression is the ability to demonstrate our thoughts, feelings, and desires and transform them. Perhaps you have some feelings and emotions that you haven't been able to simply put into words; choose a different form of expression and enjoy the process of discovery.

Self-expression allows us to visit our own edges, push our boundaries and create new ones. We can express ourselves privately and understand ourselves on a deeper level. Expression associates us back into our body, allows us to shift state, see from a different perspective and unwind the mental ball of twine, the inner workings of our mind. Flowing with our creative energy is a fantastic way to be present, improve our mood and boost self-esteem.

I challenge you to understand the impact of carving out dedicated time to express yourself, create, and prioritise and implement this. Suppose you believe that you aren't of a creative nature, and the thought of expressing your true self is frightening. In that case, I invite you to reframe these limiting beliefs and push your own edges. Find a way that feels good to you and is individual to you, enabling your beautiful, unique self to see a new way. Experiment, play, have fun and open a channel within yourself for energy to flow and shift.

By Narelle Clyde

SACRED *Self* EXPRESSION

5 *Steps* to Unleashing Your Fully Expressed Self

Being fully self-expressed is a powerful state of being where we share ourselves, unapologetically, with the world. It's a journey of embracing our true essence and breaking free from societal and generational conditioning.

But how do we become more fully self-expressed? **Here are five steps** that can help you to live a life aligned with your fully expressed self:

STEP 1 – Self-Awareness

To be more fully self-expressed, it is essential to cultivate self-awareness. This is always the first key to creating change. We must take the time to explore our inner world, the so-called good, bad and ugly. Our light and our shadow. Practices such as journaling, meditation, or engaging a life coach can help us to gain deeper insights into the wholeness of who we truly are.

These tools allow us to observe how we react in different situations and give us the awareness to explore any patterns or limiting beliefs that may be holding us back. By understanding ourselves better, we can break free from any conditioned responses and align our actions with our authentic self.

STEP 2 – Authenticity

Authenticity is the cornerstone of self-expression. When we can embrace our true self without the need for approval or validation from others, we are free! When we show up authentically, we inspire others to do the same, which in turn creates much deeper connections and intimacy with those around us.

Practice this by letting go of the masks you wear to fit in with the expectations of others and, instead, embrace your unique qualities. You'll likely find that the things you consider 'weird' about you are the very things your soul tribe will love the most.

STEP 3 – Creativity

Creativity is a powerful form of self-expression. We can cultivate this by engaging in activities that allow us to explore our creative sides. Find what resonates for you, whether it's painting, writing, dancing, singing, making music, or something else. When you were younger, what did you love to do? The activities we were drawn to as a child are often clues as to how we are designed to express ourselves in life.

Let go of any need to be 'perfect' and simply embrace creativity for the pleasure and joy that it brings.

STEP 4 – Courage and Vulnerability

There's no question that being fully self-expressed requires courage and vulnerability. It means stepping out of our comfort zone and sharing our authentic self, even when it feels very uncomfortable or uncertain. Embrace the fear of judgment and rejection, knowing that your sacred self-expression is far more important than others' opinions.

Practice by expressing yourself in small ways each day. Start by sharing your opinions in conversations when you'd usually stay quiet. Try initiating new activities with friends or your partner. Ask for what you actually need and want in life. Gradually expand your comfort zone and take bigger leaps of self-expression - it doesn't all have to happen at once!

STEP 5 – Soul Tribe

Find or create a supportive network of people who appreciate and encourage your authentic self-expression. Those who celebrate who you rather than try to dim you down to make them feel more comfortable. Seek out communities, workshops, or online groups that align with your interests and values.

A supportive environment allows you to express yourself freely without fear of judgment, fostering personal growth and self-confidence.

Ultimately, becoming more fully self-expressed is a journey of self-discovery and personal growth. By cultivating self-awareness, embracing authenticity, expressing yourself creatively, and embracing vulnerability, you can unlock the power of your true essence.

> Remember that sacred self-expression is an ongoing journey, and each step you take brings you closer to living a life aligned with who you truly are at your core.

May this serve as an invitation to embrace your wonderful uniqueness and share your beautiful light with the world.

The Science of Spirituality

THE SHARED DEATH EXPERIENCE

By Melanie Oborne

The awareness of Near-Death Experiences (NDEs) seems to outweigh that of Shared-Death Experiences (SDEs). However, these shared experiences are a critical piece of the evidential puzzle when it comes to the existence of life after death and SDE experience.

When my grandmother passed away in March of 2020, just before the pandemic hit Australia, my sister disclosed that the night before we received news of her passing, our grandmother appeared to her in a dream. She shared that this dream felt so real with our grandmother standing right in front of her and mouthing the words "I love you, goodbye". The next morning once my sister awoke, she received the news of my grandmother's death. I was deeply curious about this experience, and unbeknown to me at the time, I would later be involved in a project researching this very phenomenon. I now know what my sister experienced could be explained as a remote SDE where the experiencer is physically distant from the dying – whether they be in the next room or halfway around the world.

An experience that one or more persons may have before, during, or after death is referred to as a "shared crossing" in a wider sense. SDEs are a unique type of shared crossing that people describe as sensing, witnessing, accompanying, or even assisting in the transition of the soul or spirit of the dying to a benevolent afterlife. SDEs often happen just before or shortly after death, although they can also happen minutes, hours, days, or even weeks in advance or later. When I shared my involvement in this research with others, I often heard stories that reflected an SDE. One woman I remember disclosed to me that when she was at her father's bedside, as he was dying, she perceived mist leaving the top of his head, which she believed was his spirit leaving his body.

In an SDE, someone who is bedside or remote has experienced features that are common in NDEs. The living person might hover above their body, see a transcendent light, and perceive other deceased family members who have come to welcome the recently deceased. They may even take part in a life review with the deceased or dying person.

It is not yet known why these events occur. Could it be that the living person has instigated it somehow, or perhaps the dying person has somehow facilitated this event? Since the living individual having the SDE most definitely does not have a dying brain, the occurrence of these experiences is extremely significant since it demonstrates that some sceptical explanations for NDEs, namely that they are only hallucinations of a dying brain, may be contested.

Let's now look briefly at the research surrounding this phenomenon. The Shared Crossing Research Initiative (SCRI) performed a qualitative analysis on written accounts of semi-structured interviews with 107 participants reporting a total of 164 SDEs. This study was known to be the first of its kind in relation to end-of-life phenomena. Interestingly, over half of the participants interviewed were engaged in various types of introspective or contemplative activities such as yoga, meditation, tai chi, mindfulness etc. Could it be that these activities assist in changes in consciousness leading to the cultivation of an SDE?

The study also found that the majority of the SDE's occurred remotely, and 20 percent of participants received mental impressions such as brief thoughts, feelings and/or sensed the dying's presence. A smaller percentage of participants experienced the sudden onset of unusual physical symptoms thought to correspond to those experienced by the dying immediately before death. Over eighty percent of accounts included the appearance of unusual phenomena such as having a vision of the dying, whereby the person was described as looking younger or more vibrant (in 50 percent of the cases). Other features that highly presented, were the appearance of transcendent light, sensing energy, alterations in time and space, encounters with non-human beings, seeing light or material leave the body, appearance of previously deceased loved ones and visions of otherworldly or heavenly realms. The research is in its infancy, so the sample and population size are an obvious limitation. However, as research progresses, more can be understood about this phenomenon as this small study highlights commonalities, highlighting the need for more rigorous studies in the future.

Another important element of this study is the numerous benefits that the SDE provided, such as reconciliation of grief, loss of the fear of death and a renewed sense of meaning and purpose. Whilst it may be difficult for some to express these stories for various reasons, one being that the modern Western world has placed these experiences at the margins of supernaturalism, it is vital that people have the appropriate space to share their stories for personal validation.

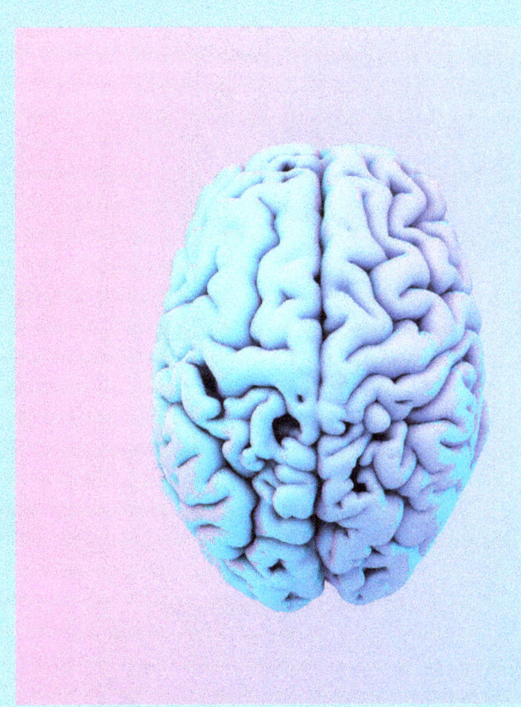

1 Shared Crossing Research Initiative (SCRI) (2021), 'Shared Death Experiences: A Little-Known Type of End-of-Life Phenomena Reported by Caregivers and Loved Ones', American Journal of Hospice & Palliative Medicine, pp. 1 – 9.

Just keep
going

Every moment is a fresh beginning.

Every beginning is a new opportunity.